The Last Shot

The Last Shot

It takes more than talent.

Why I <u>didn't</u> make it as a Pro Hockey player.

Enzo Augimeri

2005 Toronto, Canada

Enzo Augimeri
A12-1250 Eglinton Ave. W.
Suite 116
Mississauga, Ontario
L5V 1N3
CANADA
enzoaugimeri@rogers.com

Library and Archives Canada Cataloguing in Publication

Augimeri, Enzo, 1961-
    The last shot : it takes more than talent : why I didn't make it as a pro hockey player / Enzo Augimeri.

ISBN 0-9737374-0-9
1. Augimeri, Enzo, 1961- 2. Hockey players—Canada—Biography.
I. Title.

GV848.5.A94A3 2005   796.962'092   C2005-900490-8

Cover and text design: Karen Petherick, Intuitive Design International Ltd.
Illustrations: Michael Petherick
Cover photos: ©firstlight.ca

Printed and bound in Canada

DEDICATION

This book is dedicated to my father, Vincent Augimeri,
who passed away in November 1998. He provided me
with every opportunity necessary to achieve my goals.
Whether it was driving me to early morning practice
on his only day off from work, or offering guidance
after a bad game, he always made himself available.
I will always remember, and treasure,
his love and support.

ACKNOWLEDGEMENTS

I'd like to thank the following people:

My mother, who was and still is, very supportive and loving.

My wife Leena and our children Melissa and Jessie, who provide me with inspiration and motivation on a daily basis.

All my relatives, but especially my Uncle Costanzo and Uncle Italo, who took an active role in my hockey career.

Anton Thun and Howard Gourwitz, both NHL Player Agents, who helped me learn the business side of hockey.

TABLE OF CONTENTS

This book is about dreams. This book is about reality. This book is about hockey and life lessons. Like most young children playing hockey, my dream was to become a professional hockey player. For many reasons, my dream never became reality. This book shares my experiences with the reader. It details my hockey career commencing as a five-year-old playing house league up to and concluding with my years playing Junior A and University hockey in the United States and Canada. It provides young hockey players, parents and fans with an insight into a hockey career and vital lessons that are learned along the way, using my experiences as a hockey player.

This book is meant to help adolescents, young adults, and their parents. Most children and their parents have very little experience with what is really required to become a professional hockey player. The book educates the reader about the following:

- Mental preparation
- The importance of hockey practices
- The importance of strength and conditioning programs
- Being an accepted part of a team
- Fighting in hockey
- Dealing with girlfriends
- A life lesson on drugs and alcohol

- How to handle emotional situations and frustration with team management
- Playing with *Heart* and developing the proper work ethic
- The Ontario Hockey League Draft
- Playing College hockey in the United States
- Playing University hockey in Canada

One of the unique features of this book is that it presents situations that can negatively impact someone who wants to be a pro hockey player and prevent them from achieving their dream.

Most books published by former and current hockey players detail their life story and how they became professional athletes. These athletes are the exceptions. My book reveals why hockey players, like me, don't make it. There are 36 valuable lessons for the reader, outlining what they should and could be doing.

I hope this book helps you or your child to fulfill the dream of becoming a professional hockey player.

CHAPTER ONE

The Beginning

House League and Little NHL

My first game ever was at the age of five or six, playing House League in Oshawa. All I can remember is that I couldn't skate and used my hockey stick as leverage to stop myself from falling face-first onto the ice. In those days, kids my age didn't play on a full-size rink but played on half of the ice. To get into the best position to score a goal, I would park myself in front of the other team's net every time I went onto the ice.

I know we lost by a big score, maybe seven or eight to two. By the way, guess who scored the two goals for our team? I did, of course, or this book would be pretty boring. It was a great feeling to score a goal. Little did I know that there was more to this game than scoring goals.

A funny thing happened as that season progressed and my skating didn't. Early in the season, our goaltender quit the team. At practice, our coach asked for any volunteers who wanted to play net. It was as if something grabbed my arm and shot it up in the air. I had volunteered to become the new goalie for our team.

I became one of the best goalies in the league and led the team into the "A" division, where all the best teams were grouped. Whenever the puck was close to our net, I would lay down on the ice to be in position to stop the majority of shots. The only shots I wouldn't stop were when other players raised the puck off the ice. This rarely occurred. We didn't win the championship but I became a better skater lugging those pads around, and now I had a better understanding of the game.

I will share one brief story about my experience as a goalie.

I was terrified of any player who could raise the puck. You have to remember that most players at that age were lucky to make contact with the puck, let alone raise the puck off the ice. We were playing one of the better teams in the league and, like most teams, they had one player who was better than everyone else on the ice. I don't remember how many breakaways this kid had, but I do remember him closing in on me and taking his best shot. As the puck started to rise from the ice, my body froze and I closed my eyes. He scored, and they won the game 5-0. That was my first and last season of playing goal.

A few years later, at the age of eight, my play had improved and I had become one of the best and most dangerous scorers in House League. As a matter of fact, in one game I scored nine goals, and in another, believe it or not, I scored eleven goals. In the game that I scored nine goals, I could have scored more but I had to ensure that my little brother Frank, who was a teammate, got a couple of goals, or he and I would have fought that night at home.

My parents were always very supportive and enthused about my participation and progression in hockey. Although they had very little experience of or exposure to hockey, they had a big influence on my decisions – sometimes a negative influence, sometimes positive. They were born and raised in Italy and immigrated to Canada when they were in their teens. My father had played and followed soccer but was never previously exposed to hockey.

We were participating in the annual Park League tournament that was held throughout the city of Oshawa. It must have been during the winter holidays or March break, because we were playing an afternoon game. For some reason, I was at my dad's business, waiting for my mother to take me to the game. When I say waiting, I mean waiting, and waiting, and waiting. I am the type of person who thrives on being punctual; I was that way even as a kid. I was becoming increasingly frustrated, when my mother finally appeared at the front of the building. I was extremely upset even though she explained that she had to take my sister Connie to her ballet lesson and was running behind schedule.

We finally made it to the game and were surprised to see that the Zamboni was flooding the ice in what appeared to be a break between games. I raced into the dressing room and noticed that everyone, including the coach, was giving me a funny look. I apologized to the coach for being late and told him that I was glad that the game was delayed. My teammates began to laugh as the coach told me that our team had just completed the second period and were getting ready for the third and final period of the game.

 **LESSON #1**

As parents, ensure that you are aware of the dates and times of your child's games and practices. Make a concerted effort to attend and be punctual. In the event you cannot make a game or practice, provide the coach with advance notice. Obtain the names and phone numbers of other players on the team, and when necessary, arrange a ride for your child in advance. Players still have some responsibility to remind their parents when games and practices take place.

— · —

At the age of nine I tried out for "Little NHL" which was the equivalent of our modern-day rep hockey but a step below "Triple A." The leagues in Oshawa at that time were as follows:

Church or Park Leagues = House League
Little NHL = Rep
All Star = Triple A

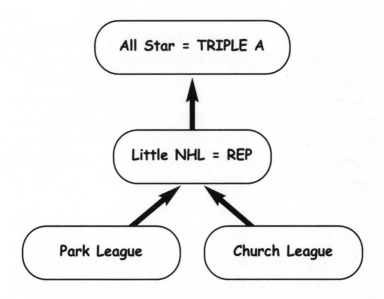

I didn't make the Little NHL Bruins hockey team. I was crushed, but I learned two great lessons: things don't always come easy and, if at first you don't succeed, try, and try again. Before trying out, I thought it would be a piece of cake, considering the fact that I was one of the best players in House League. But I was so cocky that I didn't give it my best effort, and didn't play to the best of my abilities. The result: I didn't make the team.

 **LESSON # 2**

Talent alone is not enough to become a complete hockey player. Outworking your opponent is a necessary ingredient to win the battles during the course of a game. The team with players that have superior talent will not win a game unless they match the work ethic of or work harder than their opponent. Good coaches can help you make the most of your talent but hard work must accompany the talent.

— · —

The following year, at the age of ten, I tried out for the Leafs and the Canadians (both Little NHL) at the same time. We were not supposed to try out for two teams at once and this created some controversy.

I made both teams and they both wanted me to play for them. My father somehow sorted this out after meetings with the teams and I ended up playing for the Leafs. I was so proud to put on a Maple Leaf jersey, as they were my favourite NHL team.

I did not become a force on the team until midway into the season. Being new to the coaching staff, feeling uncomfortable with my new surroundings, and not understanding that a solid effort was required, contributed to my slow start. In fact, during a tournament in Cobourg early in the season, I may have played only a couple of shifts in each of the games we played.

 **LESSON # 3**

Being benched or not playing on a regular basis is very difficult to handle. Everyone wants to be on the ice as much as possible. Try to stay positive and encourage your teammates by letting them know, with positive words or a pat on the helmet, that you are supporting them. While on the bench try to keep your legs loose by moving and shaking them as much as possible. When the opportunity comes to get onto the ice, make the most of it.

— • —

By mid-year, things began to change and I became one of the best players on the team. I started to work harder and was given the opportunity to play more. With more ice time, I began to play with more confidence, resulting in more goals and assists. That was my first and last season playing in the Little NHL, as the step up to the next level was fast approaching.

My father and mother were all smiles as I exited the dressing room and gave them the great news that I had made the triple-A team. I would now be representing the city of Oshawa as a minor peewee at the age of eleven.

CHAPTER TWO

A Hockey Player and Hockey Parents

Peewee

My parents cautioned me that although they were happy with my progression in hockey, the first priority was school. I was a good student but needed to work at it in order to maintain a B average. Playing triple-A hockey would require a commitment to the schedule of one or two practices a week and one or two games a week. Some of these games were played out of town during the week. This meant that there would be no time for homework on nights when we played on the road. I had to promise that when there were no games or practices, I would focus on my schoolwork. I would usually talk to my teachers early in the school year to let them know that doing homework some nights would be difficult.

For the most part, my teachers were very understanding and accommodating. They provided me with the home-work assignments in advance or let me hand in assignments a day late.

Once again, my development was slow (can you see a trend?), and I did not elevate my level of play until the middle of the season. It all started with a couple of familiar concepts in the sport of hockey: chemistry, and confidence.

Grove was arguably the best player on the team, and was deadly in front of the net. The coach made some line changes and Grove was now my left-winger. This was a partnership that would last for three consecutive years. I was the playmaker who unselfishly would pass the puck to Grove, even at times when I had the better oppor-tunity. I did this for the fol-lowing reasons:

1. To deliberately fake the other team.
2. To let Grove take the shot because I knew if Grove took the shot, chances were that he would score.

I was a team player. I was more concerned with winning and losing than with my own statistics. Getting an assist on a goal was just as important as scoring a goal.

Grove's claim to fame probably came during the Quebec International Peewee Hockey Tournament held annually for twelve-year-olds. It was a single-game elimination format, and our team had handily advanced to the semi-finals where we were to meet a team from Brantford. No big deal, right? Wrong. Some guy named Wayne Gretzky was playing for Brantford and was leading the tournament in scoring. In their first game, in front of approximately 14,000 people, Brantford defeated a team from Texas by a score of about 25-0! I'm not sure how many goals or assists Gretzky had but it was more than ten. Grove, on the other hand, was scoring at least a goal a game and I was creating the plays the majority of the time.

I'll never forget the atmosphere in the arena that morning. It was 8:30 a.m. on a school day and the place was packed. Our line started the game, so I lined up against Gretzky for the opening face-off. Every time we (Oshawa) touched the puck, the fans would boo. I scored our third goal early in the second period to give us a 3-2 lead, a lead we would never relinquish. The fans booed and booed. Think about it. A twelve-year-old kid who just scored a big goal in a big game, in one of the biggest tournaments around, and all he can hear is booing. This is one memory that will stick with me for the rest of my life. By the way, final score: Oshawa 8, Brantford 3. We went on to defeat another future NHL'er, Steve Larmer and his Peterborough team, 2-0 in the finals and won the tournament.

My confidence level grew as that first season progressed, but not without bumps in the road. We were playing in the first round of the Eastern Ontario playoffs and were facing Belleville in the fourth game of a best-of-five series. We were leading two games to one. I was not having one of my better games and we trailed 3-2 after two periods. Our coach decided to shorten the bench and went with two new forward lines for the third period. Unfortunately for me, I was not on either of the two lines.

We eventually won the game 5-3 and the series 3-1. With about thirty seconds left in the third period, and with little chance of a Belleville comeback, the coach put me onto the ice for the first time. As I was jumping over the boards, my father quickly approached the bench from behind and yelled at me not to go onto the ice, because if I wasn't good enough to play earlier in the third period, I wasn't good enough to play now. It's hard to explain what happened. You had to be there. My father literally leaned over the top of our bench and the only thing you could hear in the entire rink was his screaming. He said what he had to say and went back to his seat. I was completely embarrassed as my teammates and the coaching staff just stood there and looked at me. I pretended I hadn't heard him and continued to play the final shift of the game.

Later, as we drove home, he told me he wasn't happy that I went onto the ice but agreed I had no choice. He had lost his cool but felt that I was playing a pretty good game. I was one of the reasons our team had made it that far. He was angry at the coach and thought benching me wasn't the right thing to do.

LESSON # 4

Hockey-related decisions regarding a player's ability to play, ice time, and other hockey matters are made by team management. Although some management teams respect the player's opinion, it is their perception of your abilities that matters and not that of your family or friends. Even if you do not agree with the coaching philosophy, or how much ice time your child is getting, do not yell and scream at the coach, especially in public. This will only cause your child embarrassment. Meet with the coach privately and express your concerns in a diplomatic manner. Try to understand that the coach has the team's best interest in mind when making decisions.

— • —

We had made it to the Ontario finals and were playing Kitchener. (I promise this will be the last story of my first year at the Triple A level.) We were leading 3-0 in the best of seven series when Kitchener won the next two games, making it three games to two for us. Game 6 was held in Oshawa. I dominated the game at both ends of the ice, scoring three goals. We won the game 7-3. My confidence hit a new level after that game.

The following year, we participated at the major peewee level (age 12), and won the Quebec tournament.

CHAPTER THREE

The Teen Years

Bantam

Minor bantam was the most eventful year for my teammates and me during our minor-hockey careers. We were thirteen years old and our interests were changing. Where before we had only been interested in playing sports and not much else, now we began to experiment with alcohol, drugs, and dating. All of these factors contributed in one way or another to the type of season we were about to have.

I think this was the year that we played five or six tournaments and won every single one of them. The first one that comes to mind was the Peterborough tournament. We beat Peterborough in the first game and advanced after a number of other wins to the final game of the tournament.

Between the semi-final game and the final game, we went back to the hotel and were advised by our coach to take it easy and rest. One of the players on our team had a bag of marijuana (pot) with him. Six or seven of us went outside into a secluded area and smoked it. The marijuana had very little effect on me but it did have quite a negative effect on a number of the guys. Their behaviour became erratic. They became quite lethargic and had trouble focusing on playing hockey. One of the guys acted like he was drunk – I'm not sure if it was the pot or it was him trying to be funny. None of the parents or coaches noticed because it wasn't that different from his normal behaviour.

Our team played extremely well (except for some of the guys who had smoked pot) and we defeated Burlington 3-2. One of the guys on our line was outstanding and scored two goals. Our line was on the ice most of the game and even when we were two players shorthanded, our coach put my forward line onto the ice with no defencemen. I never smoked pot before a game after that.

 **LESSON # 5**

At some point or another, someone, friends
and/or teammates, may approach you to experiment
with drugs. Say no. Drugs can and will have a
negative impact not only on your hockey career,
but on all aspects of your life.

Taking drugs will impact your physical and mental well-being. Don't let others influence you: drugs are wrong. From a hockey perspective, you will not perform at your peak when you are under the influence of drugs.

— • —

We were regarded, along with Peterborough and Burlington, as one of the best teams in the Ontario Minor Hockey Association at that time. There may have been other teams who were as good, but we never encountered them. We did not, as a rule, play teams from the Metropolitan Toronto Hockey League (now the GTHL), because they had a reputation of being a "superior" league. In the finals of the Hamilton tournament, we beat the Toronto Marlies 5-0. We were regarded as underdogs going into that final game, but we took the approach that we had nothing to lose and that we could win.

 **LESSON # 6**

Games are won and lost on the ice, not on paper. Be prepared to play your opponent, and don't be intimidated because they are supposedly in a superior league or because they are ahead of you in the standings. Be confident in your team and your individual abilities. Taking the right mental approach will give you the opportunity to succeed.

— • —

We played Peterborough in the Eastern Ontario League finals that year. The series went five games and we defeated them 3-2. You could say that my mother was a factor in the outcome of Game 2. We were in Peterborough late in the third period and trailing by a couple of goals. I believe Grove scored to narrow their lead to one goal. As time wound down, I took control of the puck just outside of our blue line, near the far boards where most of the Oshawa parents were sitting. As I started to stride towards centre ice, all I could hear was my mother yelling, "Enzo, do something!" I proceeded to take the puck over the Peterborough blue line, split the defence, fake the goalie, and score the tying goal. We went on to win the game and, of course, the series. My mother, who is very petite, is not usually very vocal at games. In fact, when a game is intense and close, she will leave the rink because she becomes too nervous. I think, in this case, hearing my mother's voice inspired me to give that little extra effort that was needed.

Our minor bantam year continued and we were to meet Burlington in the Ontario semi-finals with Oshawa having the extra home game. We lost Game 3 in Oshawa, which gave Burlington a 2-1 edge in the series. We were now faced with elimination heading into Burlington for the fourth game of the series.

We showed up at practice a few days prior to Game 4 and were informed by our new coach, Grove's father, that our coach Jones, had quit. We had a very vocal group of parents who blamed Jones's unusual coaching style for the lost game. Parents were constantly complaining about their children's lack of ice time, or his unusual approach to playing three forwards when the team was two men short, or how undisciplined we had become as a team.

 **LESSON # 7**

It's the same old story: when the team is winning, the players are playing well, but when the team is losing, the easiest person to blame is the coach. Parents should remember that a coach at the minor-hockey level is a volunteer. Be patient in your assessment of the coach and his abilities. As long as your child is learning, progressing, and most importantly, having fun, then the coach is accomplishing his objectives. Having an unusual coaching style does not mean the coach cannot coach (e.g., Roger Neilson). Winning and losing should not be the only way of assessing a coach's abilities at the minor-hockey level. I once coached my daughters' soccer team, which won two games throughout the summer. In the playoffs, the team learned and progressed so much that we almost beat one of the best teams in the league, eventually losing by only one goal.

— • —

Believe it or not, we won Game 4 and headed back to Oshawa for the fifth and deciding game.

Game 5 was played in Oshawa and we were leading 2-1 with less than one minute remaining. Burlington scored with about 45 seconds left, tying the score two-all. Our line was on the ice for the tying goal and stayed on as we lined up for the face-off at centre ice. The Burlington player won the face-off cleanly from me and went around me as if I wasn't there. I had made a major mistake: when you lose a face-off you must always play the man. I didn't, and the centre-man split our defence and scored the winning goal with thirty seconds left. It was a bitter end to a very eventful season.

 **LESSON # 8**

As a centre, if you lose the face-off, it is your responsibility to stay with the opposing centre by taking the man. Tie him up and ensure your team has taken possession before letting him go.

— • —

The following year, I was a major bantam (age 14). The only significant event occurred at the very end of the season. We had eliminated Peterborough again in another five-game series and advanced to the semi-finals of the Ontario playoffs against Hamilton. Over the course of our minor hockey years, we had played Hamilton a handful of times and beaten them on every occasion. There are a couple of items to keep in mind as I relay this story. First of all, because we had never lost to Hamilton, we were definitely overconfident. Secondly, our parents had become even more vocal with the coaching and managing of our team. Thirdly, the players had become undisciplined and very outspoken about all hockey-related matters. We were questioning all the decisions that were being made and sometimes even on the bench while the game was progressing.

Game 1 was played in Oshawa, with Hamilton winning the game 8-7. We did not play very well. We were undisciplined and retaliated for Hamilton's infractions too often. As a result, we took a number of penalties. Hamilton was a very disciplined, physical team that finished their checks. We were disappointed with the result but were confident that we could go back to Hamilton and even the series.

What transpired in Hamilton in Game 2 is something that I will never forget, both from a personal and team standpoint. Until then, I had never complained about the refereeing in any game that we played. This was the worst refereeing I had ever experienced. These guys were homers, three blind mice, whatever you want to call them, but the bottom line was, they were terrible. Still, we were totally undisciplined and some of us spent the majority of the game in the penalty box. We were assessed many minor penalties and compounded the problem by taking several misconduct penalties for arguing and sometimes verbally abusing the referees.

I was always a little hot-headed and very competitive, but this may have been the turning point in my career. When I say turning point, I mean turning the wrong way rather than improving my behaviour. I took at least three or four minor penalties and two ten-minute misconducts. On one occasion, after the play had stopped and the referee was skating towards the penalty box while assessing one of my penalties, I yelled some very colourful profanity at him and blasted the puck against the boards. He looked at me, smiled, put both hands on his waist, and gave me a ten-minute misconduct. What's worse is that my teammates and I didn't take a lesson from all these penalties – we were frustrated and looking for someone other than ourselves to blame for the loss. The management team had other ideas.

LESSON # 9

Stay disciplined. Keep control of your emotions and don't let them take over. There are many instances in a period, game, or season when a teammate, opposing player, referee, fan, or coach may say or do something to upset you.
Stay cool. Focus on the task at hand. You will not play at your best unless your emotions are channeled in the proper direction. The best revenge will always be winning the game. Parents must also learn to keep their emotions in check, as their outbursts send the wrong message to kids.

— • —

A few days later, we showed up for practice to prepare for what never took place: Game 3 of the series. I was a little bit late for practice and, as I walked into the dressing room, none of my teammates were putting on their hockey equipment. They had been instructed by the coach not to put on any equipment and to wait until all the players had arrived. At the same time we were meeting with the coach, the team manager was meeting with our parents. We were told that our management team, with the support of Oshawa Minor Hockey Association, had decided to forfeit the series to Hamilton – our season was over. The coaching staff had lost control of the players and they were not willing to let anything worse happen than what had occurred in Hamilton during Game 2.

CHAPTER FOUR

Decisions, Discipline and Responsibility

Midget

I was now fifteen years old, heading into minor midget and my outlook on the game of hockey was really beginning to change. I was at the age where the focus was on either playing at a competitive and elite level for fun or trying to achieve something with the game of hockey. At fifteen, I was eligible to be selected in the Jr. A draft. Usually, not many fifteen-year-olds were selected. Most players drafted were sixteen years old, but a guy named Wayne Gretzky, was playing for the Sault Ste. Marie Greyhounds that year. Although I didn't know it at the time, my head was saying I wanted to be a professional hockey player but my heart was saying, just play for fun.

LESSON # 10

It takes many factors, including a little bit of luck, to become a professional hockey player. One of the factors you must have is HEART. You must be willing to sacrifice, pay the price, and do anything it takes to do your best. If your heart is not in it, even though your head and body may be, you will not succeed. You must want it more than anything else. Unfortunately, you can't teach someone to have heart but you can channel some people in the right direction. For example, during the 2001-2002 NHL playoffs, the Toronto Maple Leafs suffered a number of injuries to some of their top players. They still managed to defeat the Ottawa Senators in seven games, not because they were more skillful but because they were more determined and played with heart.

— • —

Nowadays, the Ontario Hockey League junior draft is conducted annually for fifteen-year-olds (minor midget) during the month of May. Players are rated by the league's scouts (Central Scouting), and these ratings are distributed to teams over the course of the year. But it is the team's ratings of each individual player, and not Central Scouting's ratings, that determine when a player will be drafted. The draft is conducted via tele-conference, with the team that finished in last place the previous season having the first selection. The draft continues until all teams, in order of last to first, have had an opportunity to select a player. Once each team has selected a player, the "round" has been completed. The draft will last up to a maximum of 15 rounds.

I didn't do anything special to prepare myself for the year during the off-season and it showed. Things started out slowly again. I noticed that a number of the elite players on the other teams, guys that I had played against for years, were becoming physically stronger and faster. What I didn't know then is that some players began working at on- and off-ice conditioning programs during the summer. This was their way of working towards becoming better hockey players and getting that little extra edge that is required in order to win the battles on the ice. My parents and I were inexperienced with the process and never thought to ask for advice. We could have explored several different avenues in order to get the proper advice. We could have spoken to one or a combination of the following people or organizations:

- Oshawa Minor Hockey
- The management of the Oshawa Generals
- Players who had competed at the Junior and/or NHL level
- A player agent
- Strength and conditioning professionals

I was always ready for big games and usually played well in them. This was not the case in our first big game of the year. We played a team from Chicago early one Sunday morning at the Children's Arena in Oshawa. Nowadays, teams from Ontario play teams from the United States on a regular basis. In the seventies, that was not the case, so this was considered a big game. I played poorly due to a number of factors, mostly of my own doing. The arena was extremely cold and I was not mentally sharp, plus it was an early morning game. In addition, I had stayed out late with some friends the previous evening.

LESSON # 11

Mental and physical preparation is extremely important. You must focus on the task at hand at all times, and don't let any external pressures or the environment affect that focus. Take the necessary time before a hockey game to concentrate on what you need to do during the course of the game to play your best. Think about different situations and how you should react to them. Do not worry about how cold the arena is, or if all of your family and/or friends are in attendance. Ensure that you warm up prior to the game by stretching. Get the blood flowing in your body prior to stepping onto the ice. If your body doesn't feel like playing, and this happens from time to time, get involved early in the game by hitting someone or taking a hit to get the emotions flowing. Consult with the appropriate professionals so your body is physically prepared before and during the season to ensure you have the ability to play at your best.

— · —

The highlight of my minor hockey career came during a game against a touring team from Sweden.

We played at the Children's Arena in Oshawa where, again, it was cold but that didn't matter this time. The arena was jammed and you could not find a place to sit or stand anywhere. My grandparents and a number of my aunts and uncles journeyed from Toronto to see the game. They would not be disappointed.

I talked about the importance of mental preparation earlier and this was probably why my play rose to new heights during this particular game. Before the game, in the dressing room, all I could focus on was what I needed to do in order to play well and win the game. I was anxious and it showed. I remember becoming upset because one of my teammates was taking too long with the tape. I needed to tape my socks and couldn't wait for him to finish.

The Swedes were extremely fast, which was not one of my strong points. I was a player who "thought the game" well, anticipated the play, and was usually in the right position at the right time. During this particular game, I compensated for my lack of speed with intensity. The Swedes went ahead early before I scored prior to the end of the first period. In the second period, it was all Sweden: they took a commanding 3-1 lead heading into the third period. The coaches must have realized that I was having a super game because they kept putting me on the ice in different situations.

Early in the third period, I stole the puck from a Swedish defender near the face-off dot in the Swedish end, skated in front of the net, and scored. The score was now 3-2 for Sweden, and it stayed that way until very late into the third period. We were playing four skaters a side, with less than two minutes remaining in the game. The puck was loose just outside the Swedish blue line. The Swedish defenceman and I raced for the puck. My intensity prevailed. I bounced the puck off the boards around him and avoided his check. I was on an angle, alone on a clear-cut breakaway from their blue line, so I cut slowly towards the middle of the net as I approached their goalie. I dragged the puck towards my skates as I started to angle towards the far side of the net. I quickly shot the puck waist-high at the part of the net I had just passed. The net bulged as the puck hit the back of it. The place erupted and all of my teammates came off the bench to celebrate the tying goal. The final score was 3-3. I had scored all three goals and was named the game's most valuable player.

The next day the sports section of the *Oshawa Times* was very complimentary to me. Did it go to my head? Of course it did. For the rest of the season, I played well but not at the level I experienced during that one particular game. I needed to continue playing at that level to become the best player I could be.

 **LESSON # 12**

You are only as good as your last shift. Never rest on your laurels. Just because you played well in the previous game or on the previous shift doesn't mean you can relax. By relaxing or thinking that things will come easily, you will not play at your best. You must work hard and play like it is your last opportunity to do something each and every time it is your turn to go on the ice.

— · —

I was sixteen years old. I hadn't been drafted but that summer I did receive an invitation from the Oshawa Legionnaries Junior B hockey club to attend their training camp. A handful of other players from our team had also been invited. I was in reasonably good shape when training camp came because I had skated periodically throughout the summer. I was still unaware that strength was a key factor as players progressed to the junior level. Again, I hadn't prepared my body properly.

Training camp was conducted during the long weekend prior to the beginning of the school year. I played extremely well in the two scrimmages in which I participated and left the rink feeling good about my chances to progress to the next stage of training camp. However, prior to the next practice, I was informed that I did not make the team and that I was to report to the Oshawa major midget hockey team. I was disappointed but not crushed.

LESSON # 13

Players should play at a level where their skills and talents are challenged. To get better and learn, you play with and against the best. Some players are not challenged at a lower level, and may pick up bad habits. For some players who excel, it becomes a difficult decision whether to move to the junior level or stay at the bantam or midget level. If a player is physically ready and gets the necessary ice time, there is nothing wrong with playing at an advanced level of hockey. However, it should be noted that the player must be capable of playing at that level. If the player is not physically ready and/or is only going to get a few shifts a game at the advanced level, he is better off not moving up.

In order for a player to improve, he or she must get a regular turn (every third or fourth shift) on the ice. Limited ice time will be of no use to players at the age of 15 or 16, and might negatively impact their confidence level. In addition, players moving up will be playing with athletes as much as four or five years older than them. They will no longer be playing with friends their own age, and this can be a challenge both mentally and physically. Older players who are not focussed on a hockey career (they're focussed on having a good time) can have a negative impact on a younger player, on and off the ice. Make sure when the younger players make the jump to the next level, they are ready.

— • —

I was indifferent after being released by the Junior B team and playing midget hockey because I felt I was ready to play at the next level. It showed in my performance – my major midget year may have been my worst as a minor-hockey league player. Remember, this was my draft year, and if I wanted to advance to Junior A, I needed to show the scouts that I was capable of playing at that level.

One event early in the season sticks out in my mind. We were playing in Trenton one Sunday afternoon and, when we played on the opposing team's rink, games were usually a lot more physical. I was not a physical player. I was a skilled player who tried to play the game with finesse. One reason I wasn't physical was that I was an average-size kid; also, I wasn't as strong as other hockey players because I didn't work at it. The game was becoming physical, and I started to retaliate by slashing and whacking at the opposing players every chance I got. After one stoppage of play near the boards, I heard my manager yell something about the way I was playing. I turned and yelled some obscenities at him. I realized I was wrong as I skated back to the bench at the end of my shift.

After the game, our manager scolded me in the hallway for about ten minutes. I didn't say a word because I knew he was right. I had let my emotions get the better of me again. I was beginning to develop a negative reputation for being hot-headed and vocal about my opinions. I believe this had an impact on my career.

We were defeated by Peterborough 3-2 that season in the Eastern Ontario League finals, but not without a fight. Playing Peterborough was always fun for me, and I played my best hockey of the season in that series. We were down 2-0 and went to Peterborough for Game 3 facing elimination.

I scored once and set up two other goals for a 3-1 win. The next day in Oshawa we defeated Peterborough 6-3. I scored two goals and assisted on a couple of others.

Game 5 was played in Peterborough the following day and we were defeated by a score of 5-0. I thought after that game my season was over.

As a precaution in case players were injured, three or four players from our team, including myself, received the phone call that we were to report to the Oshawa Jr. B hockey team for their playoffs. I was excited but I knew that I would get limited ice time, if any. We played Markham in the first round and I played on the fourth line. We received a limited amount of ice time and I scored in one of the games. We won the series 4-0.

Pickering was our next opponent and I did not play in any of the games. It was a very physical series, which may have been the reason why the midget players did not participate. We won the series and advanced to the Metro Junior B league finals against St. Michaels. I don't remember how or why or when it occurred but, as the series progressed, I started to dress for games and was an instrumental member of the team's third line.

Mike Keenan, who later went on to a great coaching career in the NHL, gave me the opportunity to play regularly. I rewarded him with some fine play but, on one occasion, my laziness cost us a game and may have made him think twice about playing me.

The game was tied late in the third period and, with less than two minutes remaining in the game, our line was on the ice. We had kept the puck in the St. Michael's end for a long period of time and were quite fatigued. Before we had an opportunity to get to the bench for a change,

St. Mike's broke out on a three-on-two rush when our line got caught a little too deep in their zone. I was behind their centreman and as we crossed centre ice I was close enough to catch him. As they crossed our blue line, their left-winger took the pass and stayed wide on our defenceman. As he approached the face-off circle in our end, he chipped a pass to their centreman, who fired the puck past our goalie for the winning goal. How did I mess up, you ask? I hadn't made the extra effort to catch that centreman. In fact, as he crossed our blue line, I began to glide (lazy, lazy, lazy!) and probably had the best seat in the house to watch him score the goal. Mike not only blasted me but my linemates as well when we got back to the bench.

 **LESSON # 14**

Give your best effort at all times. Even when you are tired, you should never stop trying. Hockey is a team game and your teammates are relying on you. Make a determined effort to use any resources you have in order to get the job done. Remember, your shifts should last approximately thirty to forty-five seconds. If a shift lasts longer, make sure you work through being tired, and do whatever you must to stop an opposing player and get the necessary stoppage of play by freezing or icing the puck. If you cannot freeze or ice the puck, do whatever possible to get the puck into the other team's end, so that you can get to the bench and make the appropriate change.

— · —

For some reason, Mike had confidence in me and played me on the third line in the seventh and deciding game against St. Michaels for the Metro Junior B championship. He even put me on the ice for a power play when they were two men short. I want to say here and now that Mike was the best coach I ever had, though I didn't realize it until later in life. By the way, we won the game and the championship. Next stop, Stratford.

The Ontario Junior B semi-finals began in Oshawa. We beat the junior team from Stratford 8-7, and if memory serves, I scored once and assisted on at least one or two other goals.

Game 2 of the series was played in Stratford. The arena seats around one thousand people, but the unusual part about this arena is that the ice surface is extremely small. (I could almost imagine what the Montreal Canadiens or the Toronto Maple Leafs must have felt when they played in Boston or Buffalo on the smaller ice surfaces compared to the old Montreal Forum or Maple Leaf Gardens.) In addition, there was an Indian chief, or at least a guy dressed up as an Indian chief, parading around on the ice prior to the game. One more thing, and this was new to me, many fans held plastic containers full of coins and they shook them in unison to make a loud noise throughout the game. My dad had made the drive to Stratford along with a few of my buddies, and they were overwhelmed by the experience.

I had a ton of ice time that game. At one point in the second period, a line brawl broke out and most of our top five players, and theirs, were ejected from the game. We lost that game and the next three as well. We were eliminated by Stratford in five games.

At the team banquet a few weeks later, I was talking to Coach Mike and told him how much I was looking forward to the upcoming season. Believe it or not, I really was. Mike's confidence in me was like a breath of fresh air and had given me a new outlook on hockey. He told me that he didn't expect me to be back with the Junior B team next season. He thought that I would be drafted and could make a Junior A club.

CHAPTER FIVE

Loneliness, Peer Pressure and Drinking

Jr. B

I had mixed emotions when Vince, the Manager of the Oshawa Generals, left a message with my parents that, at the age of seventeen, I had been drafted in the eleventh round by the Junior A team. On the one hand, if I made the Generals, I would have the opportunity to play for my home team and continue to live in the comfortable surroundings of my house. I could still hang out with my friends, visit my relatives, and attend the same high school. And I would be playing on the same junior team that Bobby Orr had played on. On the other hand, I felt that there would be a lot of pressure, playing in my hometown, and that I would be under the microscope more than any other player. In addition, it would be harder to bond with the players because the guys on the team usually hung out with each other. I was used to spending most of my time with my high-school friends and my relatives.

I had anticipated being drafted by one of the other teams in the league. Expectations in a different city would not be as high as in my hometown. I would have the opportunity for a fresh start in new surroundings, on a new team and at a new high school. I would be staying with a local family, probably with one of my teammates as a roommate. It would give me the opportunity to "grow up" and bond with my new teammates.

A couple of weeks after being drafted, I received a welcome package in the mail from the Generals that included a conditioning program. By the end of the summer, in addition to the required weight training, players were required to run three miles per day for the month of July (except Sundays) and five miles per day for the month of August (except Sundays). My father and I were not experienced with off-ice conditioning programs and I didn't take the package as seriously as I should have. By the end of the summer, I was able to run three or four miles but not within the required time. I did some weight training but nothing close to the required amount. I was inexperienced, immature, and maybe a little lazy. Being with my friends and having a good time was priority number one.

Labour Day weekend in September was the official beginning of Junior A training camp throughout Ontario. The Generals were no exception. Thursday prior to the weekend we had our physicals and I passed without any problems. On Friday morning we had our first off-ice conditioning session and I was able to pass all the required tests. Friday afternoon, I took to the ice with a number of other hopefuls for our first scrimmage and played, to my surprise, extremely well. The one thing that I did do over that summer was skate as often as I could. I know I was on the ice twice per week for the month of August. I felt comfortable and confident on the ice. On Saturday we had two on-ice sessions, as well as one on early Sunday morning. Again, things went extremely well. I was focussed, relaxed, and comfortable just playing hockey. I had no real expectations since I had been drafted so low. This probably helped me play well.

After the Sunday morning session, the team was to make several cuts and I was nervous that I would be one of them. My father told me that an NHL scout who had been watching training camp told him on the Saturday that I would make the team, but that didn't ease my tension.

I made the first cut and prepared for the annual Red and White game held on the first Monday night of training camp. I played extremely well again and felt confident heading into my first pre-season game, which was to be held the following evening at home against the Peterborough Petes.

Fighting, physical play, and what seemed like war dominated my first Junior A pre-season game. The game of hockey had changed. Players were bigger, faster, stronger, and, what I had never noticed before, meaner. Every time I touched the puck on my first shift, I got banged. In fact the very first time I touched the puck, a Peterborough player slashed my hand so hard I thought it was going to fall off. I was confused and startled by the intensity and aggression of the opposing team. It seemed that the first thought on every Peterborough player's mind was to take the man first, not the puck, and take him hard. In addition, there were several fights over the course of the game, and that was something I was not used to. It was a long evening for me as I struggled the entire game.

LESSON # 15

Different players and teams play different styles and can sometimes adjust during the course of a game, or for a certain opponent. Learn to make the minor adjustments necessary in order to play your game. Do not let the opponents intimidate you. Once they do, you will not be at your best. Don't worry about them; ensure they worry about you.

— • —

The entire pre-season was a struggle and I went from being one of the favourites to make the team, to being a long shot. Everything appeared to rest on the final road trip of the pre-season – a trip to play teams in the Quebec Junior A league. We were scheduled to play Cornwall and then Hull the following evening.

I was seventeen years of age and my first priority was to have fun. It should have been hockey and school, but it wasn't. *No one told me to, and I can't remember why I did it, but I purchased a small bottle of rye whiskey prior to leaving on the road trip. I hid it in my travelling bag. We* played Cornwall the first game of the trip and I got limited ice time, playing only so-so because I couldn't get my head into the game. Since the regular season was just around the corner, our coach wanted to put the line combinations together that would be starting the season.

After the game, we boarded the bus and arrived at our Ottawa hotel around 9 p.m. With my fate as a Junior A hockey player resting on these two games, I should have relaxed at the hotel, focussed on preparing for the next game, and gone to bed at a decent hour. Instead, I drank the entire bottle of whiskey and hopped in a cab with several of the other players headed for a bar across the river in Hull, Quebec.

The bar was jumping that night and, along with several of the guys, I had a number of beers and left around two in the morning. I arrived back at the hotel loaded and went straight to bed.

I woke up the next day with a terrible hangover, vomiting, and with a splitting headache. Most of the guys who were at the bar had not been as drunk as I was. I wanted to be part of the team. I thought hanging out with the guys and having a few beers was the way to become accepted.

We played that evening and boarded the bus for home right after the game. Needless to say, I may have played my worst game ever, and my fate was sealed.

LESSON # 16

Never drink excessive amounts of alcohol the night before a game. In fact, never drink excessive amounts of alcohol. Your mind and body are your most important and effective tools when playing the game of hockey. When playing at an elite level, you are required to be in top physical condition throughout the entire season. When you drink alcohol, your body will not respond appropriately and you will not perform at your best. I understand that players at the junior level like to indulge in having a few beers after a game. But be responsible. The legal drinking age in Ontario is nineteen. The problem with social drinking is a few beers can lead to a few more beers, and then a few more beers. Do not get into the bad habit of drinking too much and too often. And definitely do not drink and drive.

— · —

Reading it in a newspaper should not be the way you find out your fate with a junior hockey club. This is exactly what happened a few days after returning from our Quebec games. I would usually go home after school for a light snack, read the sports section of the *Oshawa Times* and head out for practice. Regardless of how well or how poorly I was playing, I was still hopeful that I would be a member of the Oshawa Generals for the upcoming season. Imagine my shock when I read in the *Times* that the Oshawa Generals had trimmed their roster and were sending Enzo Augimeri down to their Junior B hockey club.

As usual, I arrived at the Civic Auditorium about forty-five minutes prior to the start of practice. Upon my arrival, one of the trainers advised me to talk to Vince, who was in the coach's office. He told me that I was one of the biggest surprises at training camp, and had come very close to making the team. He felt that I wasn't quite ready to play at that level and that a season playing Junior B would be good for me. I said very little but experienced a series of emotions: I was mad at the Generals for telling the newspaper of my fate before telling me, disappointed at not making the hockey club, and mad at myself for not playing my best.

You see and read it all the time that an NHL player has been sent to the minors. The advice they are given is to work hard and they may be back with the big club before the season ends. Unfortunately, I did not take this approach and it showed in my performance. My season with the Junior B club began slowly. My attitude to the game was that I didn't have to work that hard. After all, I was one of the last players released from the Generals, and all I had to do was show up at the Junior B level and things would work out great. I was absolutely, one hundred percent wrong.

Although I did play on the second-best line on the team, I was probably averaging only a point per game until more than a quarter of the way into the season when we made some line changes. I was grouped with two older wingers who were in their third year in the league and were very good hockey players. Without knowing it, my game started to improve and, as my game improved, my work ethic began to change as well. I started working harder, not only during games but in practices as well. Again, chemistry and confidence began to make the difference. Still, players were being called up periodically to the Generals and I was not one of them. This made me mad and gave me added incentive to work harder.

I remember playing the North York Flames in the east end of Toronto one evening. They were a big and physical team, but I was in the right frame of mind and played a great game. The first period was scoreless, although both teams had several good scoring chances. Midway in the second period, I stole the puck from a North York player at our blue line, skated up ice, and fired a slap shot just as I approached their blue line. Even though I had probably the worst shot on the team, that shot was a rocket. It went high into the top corner of the net, over the outstretched glove of the goalie. I was shocked, but we now led 1-0 and that was all that mattered.

LESSON # 17

Work on your shot. This can easily be accomplished during and after the hockey season. Set up an area in the garage, backyard, or basement of your house, where you can shoot pucks at either a piece of plywood or against the wall. Shoot as often as possible. When given the opportunity before, during, or after practice, shoot pucks at the net. Try to develop a hard and accurate shot. There have been average hockey players who have gone on to stardom because they can put the puck in the net. Scoring is a skill that cannot be taught, but having a hard and accurate shot can be.

— • —

After the game, our coach, Mike, introduced me to a scout from United States International University, San Diego, California. He was impressed with my play and informed me that the university might be interested in me playing for them the following season. He said we would talk at a later date. Wow, was I excited! Not only was there a possibility for a scholarship, but I could be playing hockey in San Diego, California. How great would that be? I made a number of poor choices while playing hockey, but when I reflect on my opportunities, this is definitely the one that got away.

At this point, it's important to explain the different options that players had at that time and how things worked. The following options were available for 15- and 16-year-old midget players:

1. They could play Junior B or Tier 2 Junior A and attempt to obtain a scholarship from an American university. (This still applies today.)
2. They could play Junior A hockey in Canada, but would not then be eligible to obtain a scholarship from an American university. The NCAA (National Collegiate Athletic Association), the governing body for university sports in the United States, did not allow players to participate at the Junior A level and then play in the NCAA, and still does not. Players still had the option of attending and playing at a university in Canada if they were unsuccessful in their attempts to get into pro hockey. Nowadays, if a player is not offered a pro contract, his Junior A team will pay for a portion of his Canadian university education, depending on the junior contract negotiated.
3. The third option available was to sign a "school package" contract (not available today). Players could still play Junior A hockey but would not be paid. This way, they would remain eligible to receive a scholarship from an American university.

School was going well but continued to be a challenge due to my commitment to hockey. I was now in Grade 12 and managed to maintain a B average (70-75%). Our schedule involved practising every Tuesday and Thursday after school for about one-and-a-half hours and playing games twice a week. Most of the games were played on the weekend so there was time for homework after practices during the week.

My performance started to get better and better. I was scoring in bunches and was approaching the top ten goal scorers in the league. Nothing could go wrong and everything went right.

It happened as we were changing after practice one evening. Mike came into the dressing room to let us know that the Generals were calling up a few players. My name was the last to be announced and my heart was pumping at high speed. I was thrilled when I went home and told my parents but I didn't have a lot of time to relish the moment. The following evening the Oshawa Generals were in Kingston to play the Kingston Canadians.

CHAPTER SIX

Work Ethic and Distractions

Jr. A

I had played at Kingston's main arena during my minor-league days, so being at that arena did not feel unusual. The dressing room was small, cramped, and old. The Generals were a good team, but not one of the better teams in the league, although there were several players on the team that later went on to have NHL careers. That evening in the dressing room, the following future NHL players were there: Tom McCarthy, Charlie Huddy, Greg Stefan, Lee Norwood, Rick Lanz, and Steve Konroyd.

I only played four or five shifts that night, but I represented myself well and was given the opportunity to play two nights later at the Civic Auditorium in Oshawa against the Sault Ste. Marie Greyhounds.

Have you ever played, or imagined your son/daughter playing, the game of your/their career? Well, I did it twice. The first time was as a minor-league player against the Swedish team. The second was my first league game at the Civic Auditorium in Oshawa as a member of the Oshawa Generals, playing against the Greyhounds.

Mental preparation, determination, confidence, and intensity are key components for hockey players but the *Number One* quality you must have is the ability to compete.

 **LESSON # 18**

The Scholastic Children's Dictionary defines "compete" as "to try hard to outdo others at a task, race or contest." In hockey, one of the words scouts use most often is "compete." Does a player compete night in and night out? I define "compete" in hockey terms as giving 100% effort every shift of the entire game, and being willing to do whatever it takes to win within the rules of the game. The competitive player is willing to battle through checks, sacrifice his body, and work as hard as possible. In order to make it as a pro, a hockey player must, and I mean must, compete every shift of every game. Compete with consistency.

— · —

I competed my butt off that evening in Oshawa. I wish I could have maintained that intensity all of the time, but only rarely did I compete with the intensity that was required to play Junior A hockey. It's easy to prepare mentally for a big game. It was my first Junior A game in my hometown. My parents, friends and family were all watching. Factors such as the temperature in the rink, how my body felt, and where the party was that night were not important. The only important factor was playing well and winning.

My line was on the ice for the opening face-off. Thirty seconds into the game, the Greyhounds scored. With my head down and my shoulders slouched, I headed towards our bench but was told to stay on the ice. I won the face-off and our defenceman crossed centre ice and shot the puck into the Soo (Sault Ste. Marie) zone. One of my wingers won a battle for the puck from a Soo defender and passed the puck back to our defenceman at the point. I made my way to the front of the net and waited for the shot to either tip it or screen the goalie. It was a low shot headed for the far corner but at the last second the Soo goalie stuck out his skate and made a terrific save.

I have watched a number of sports movies that slow the scene down when the most important play of the games occurs. I know it didn't really happen, but when the puck rebounded off the goalie's skate onto my stick in front of the net, it was like everything around me stopped. I was alone in front of the net facing a goalie on one side of the net on his knees. I faked to my left and backhanded the puck into the open side of the net. As I started to raise my arms in celebration, I looked up and saw my dad's face peering between two spectators at the top of the arena. My dad passed away a couple of years ago but his expression that day will remain etched in my mind forever. After the game, my dad told me that he had arrived late but was just in time to see the puck slide into the net. My mother was behind him and was disappointed that she didn't see my goal.

From that point on, I did very little wrong and many things right. My first assist in the game came early in the second period and exemplified exactly what intensity and competing is all about. I managed to keep the puck in the Soo zone at their blue line, close to the boards. As I turned up the ice, a Soo player bounced me hard against the boards. I felt a surge of determination as I bounced off the boards, pushed the Soo player away and continued along the boards in their zone. There was no one to pass the puck to, so I continued along the boards until I reached the end of the rink and turned towards the net behind the red line. A second Soo defender bounced me hard against the boards, and again I pushed the player aside as if there was no one there. As I approached the side of the net, a third Soo defender leaned on me and tried to take the puck from my stick. I managed to pass the puck to one of my wingers streaking through the slot who one-timed the puck into the back of the net. It was sheer determination on my part that produced that goal.

The game ended in disappointment with a final score of 6-5 for the Greyhounds. However, I had accomplished two things that night – I had proved to the Oshawa

Generals that I was capable of playing at that level, and I had gained the confidence that every player must have to play at their best.

Our next game took place on a Saturday afternoon in Oshawa against the Sudbury Wolves. The Generals were battling the Wolves for second place in the division, so this game was huge. I was still a member of the Legionnaires, but continued being used as a "call-up" while some of the General players were recovering from injury. I still participated in the Legionnaries games as long as there were no conflicts in the schedule. I had played the previous evening with the Junior B team and managed to score three goals. Fatigue was not a factor because I was so excited. I had a goal and two assists as we beat the Wolves 6-3.

A couple of days later, before practice with the Legionnaires, Mike called me into his office for a meeting. He advised me that the Generals wanted me to play with them for the remainder of the season. He carefully explained the options that I had in relation to playing Junior A, the school package, and a university scholarship in the United States. He didn't try to convince me to stay with his club but advised me of my options and suggested I talk it over with my parents. At the age of seventeen, I was faced with a decision that would determine my future, just as many players at the age of fifteen or sixteen face today.

My dad wasn't always right but on this occasion he was. My mother and I heard what he was saying but didn't really listen. He was convinced that if I continued to play the way I was playing at the Junior B level, I would have the choice of accepting one of a number of U.S. scholarship offers. He was being realistic, stating that as a player who was only five-feet ten-and-a-half-inches tall, one-hundred-

and-sixty-five-pounds, and a below average skater who lacked the toughness required to consistently play in the traffic at the Junior A level, I was better off working towards a scholarship. We didn't listen to him. We told him that this could be my opportunity to make it to the NHL. *We were wrong.* My dad felt that if I worked on my skating in the off seasons and followed a weight-training program, I could possibly have a shot at the NHL after earning a degree. Again, he was right. My mother and I felt that playing in the junior league from which the majority of NHL teams drafted their players was my best option. The discussion went on for many hours that evening and ended with my mother and I having our way.

 **LESSON # 19**

The choice between playing Junior A hockey, or playing Junior B/Tier 2 hockey and working towards a U.S. scholarship, is difficult. If drafted by a Junior A hockey club, do your research and find out as much about the organization as possible. Based on your draft position, you can negotiate a certain amount of money towards your tuition at a Canadian university if you do not sign a pro contract. (This includes the American and East Coast hockey leagues). Meet with the organization (accompanied by your parents and/or an agent) to get an understanding of the direction the team is heading and where you fit into their plans. Talk to current and former players to get a perspective on how they have been treated by the organization.

Visit the city and talk to the local educators to determine educational needs. Find out if there is a university or college in the city, or a satellite location, to continue post-secondary education. Talk to the coach. Try to get an understanding of what style of play he prefers and what type of system he uses. Meet with prospective billets (people you may live with) to ensure their lifestyle will assist, or at least not hinder, your aspirations, and will provide you with a proper environment to play hockey and continue your studies. Obtain a number of objective opinions of your ability and your potential for becoming an NHL player. Are you a pro prospect? Make an informed decision by doing your homework!

— · —

The choice should have been easy. The following is a list of questions that players and families should ask themselves, and my own self-evaluation at that time:

- Skating ability? *Below average*
- Toughness? *Not physical or tough*
- Competitiveness? *Did not compete on a consistent basis*
- Face-off ability? *Excellent*
- Playmaking ability? *Excellent*
- Understanding of the game? *Extremely smart with and without the puck*
- Goal Scorer? *Average*
- Teamwork? *Great team player*
- Size? *Below average*

I made the decision to play Junior A hockey with the Oshawa Generals. I should have continued my Junior B career and accepted a scholarship to an American university where I could have developed my skills and focussed on my education. My skills and abilities at the time were better suited to doing that. However, the decision was made and life moved on. I was ready to take the next step towards my goal of playing hockey in the NHL.

Present-day Hockey-Level Pyramid

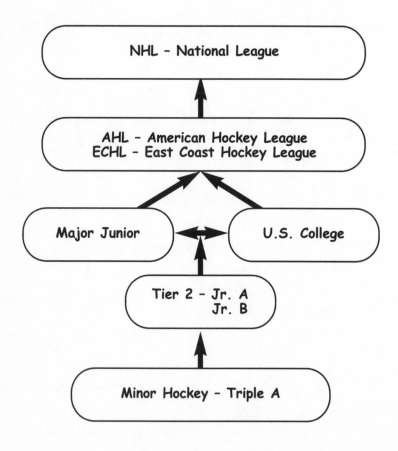

My first official game as a General was a couple of nights later in Peterborough against the first place Petes. I was placed on a line with Tom and Diego. Tom was a genuine pro prospect, our leading scorer, and probably the best offensive player on our team. Diego had an average amount of skill but he was also our enforcer. It was evident that it was Diego's job to take care of Tom and me if things started getting out of hand.

It was a tight, low-scoring, physical hockey game. I was mentally prepared and played very well that evening. With the score tied 1-1 (I had assisted on Tom's goal), I won a face-off in the Peterborough zone back to our defenceman at the point. He drilled a shot that the Petes' goalie stopped with his blocker. The puck lay in front of the net and I pounced on it before anyone else could. I skated right by the sprawled goaltender and backhanded the puck into the top corner of the open side of the net.

The game remained 2-1 for us very late into the third period. There was about a minute left in the game with a face-off in our zone and Peterborough had pulled their goalie for an extra attacker. The coach put our line on the ice and gave me the task of taking the very important face-off. Although I had developed into a premier face-off man in previous leagues, this was only my fourth Junior A game. I was nervous but I knew our coach had a great deal of confidence in me, or he would have used one of our other centremen. I lost the draw and the puck went back to the Peterborough defenceman at the point. He drilled a shot that hit our goalie's chest and rebounded in front of the net. A mad scramble occurred for about twenty seconds until I was flattened onto the ice by a Petes' forward with the puck underneath me. The referee blew his whistle and stopped the play. Then I learned a very important lesson. As I slowly started to get up, one of our defencemen hovered over me as the play stopped and told me not to get up. I didn't understand what he meant. He looked directly into my eyes and, without raising his voice, told me again not to get up. I still didn't understand what he meant. As I continued to rise, no one saw him shove me back onto the ice and yell at me not to get up. I finally understood what he meant!

Throughout my entire hockey career to this point, I had never pretended to be hurt and, in fact, had missed very few games due to injury. Our defenceman wanted me to fake an injury so that the players on the ice could get a break and meet with the coach while the trainer attended to my needs.

Our trainer understood exactly what was happening and asked the appropriate questions to an injured player. The referee probably understood as well but there was nothing he could really do. A couple of players and the trainer assisted me off the ice and I went directly to our dressing room. Fifteen seconds later I was back on the bench, watching in utter frustration as Peterborough tied the score with less than twenty seconds left in the game.

On the very first shift of overtime, I took a pass from Diego and immediately slid the puck to Tom. He took a slap shot that fluttered over the goalie's right shoulder and into the net for the winning goal.

It was a big win, not only for me but also for the team. This was the General's first win against the Petes all season. After the game, the coaching staff and most of the players congratulated me on my performance. Not only had I scored a goal and two assists, but it was also the third consecutive game that I had scored in. Three goals and six assists after four games with the Generals – those were awfully impressive statistics for a rookie. The guys were very friendly with me on the ride home in the bus and I started to feel like I was part of the team. A few of the guys came up to me and started asking questions about my hockey career. They took a real interest in me and that made me feel very accepted. For any player, being respected and being "one of the guys" is an important part of being on a team.

The following night, we played the Ottawa 67's in Ottawa. We lost the game 8-0. I played an average game, allowing my mind to wander and my eyes to gaze at the arena and the large crowd. Ottawa's arena was the second-largest rink in the province, seating approximately 11,000 people. The attendance that night was only about 5,500 but, after an incident in the second period, it felt like the place was full.

As in most visiting rinks, the fans behind the bench can get very annoying and obnoxious. I can't remember what upset this particular fan, but after the play had stopped, he began screaming and banging on the glass behind our bench. As the glass started to shake, one of our defencemen got caught up in the moment and started screaming back at him. The screaming intensified as the fan pretended to climb the glass to get at the player. Our player totally lost his cool and did one of the stupidest things a player could do. He swung his stick over the glass and just missed the head of a boy who was probably not older than eight. The fans closest to the boy reacted very angrily to the incident and were ready to take matters into their own hands. The security guards and police reacted immediately to avoid what could have been a very bad scene.

On a Sunday evening two nights later, we played the Petes in Oshawa. Once again I let the atmosphere get the best of me and I spent a great deal of the game gazing at the stands to see who was in attendance. I could tell you that everyone was there to see me, but then I would be exaggerating. The place was full because we were playing the Petes, who were in first place. I played an average game and we lost for the second game in a row.

The following weekend we were back at it after three consecutive days of practice. We left on Wednesday evening, immediately after practice, for our northern road trip to Sault Ste. Marie and Sudbury. We arrived in Sudbury that night and were to play the Greyhounds in Sault Ste. Marie the following evening and the Wolves in Sudbury on Friday night.

In Sault Ste. Marie I was firing on all cylinders and scored three goals in the game. We won 11-3 with me scoring my first and only Junior A hat trick. The following evening in Sudbury, we won 6-5 and I had another goal. My point total and playing time were increasing. I had scored six goals and recorded six assists in eight games as a rookie in the league.

This should have been the start of something great. My performance and production should have been improving. I was scoring at a sizzling pace and my game was at an all-time high. I needed to work on my skating and get a lot stronger so that I could win battles along the boards and in front of the net. I needed to stay focussed on playing hockey and ensure that I was mentally prepared to play each and every shift. I needed to prioritize my studies and hockey before having fun and being with my girlfriend. I needed to play with heart and passion, just as I had been over the past month with the Legionnaires and Generals.

When I look back now, I can't believe how well I played in those first few games with the Generals. I'm sure that one or two pro scouts circled my name on the lineup sheets as they watched those games. I was a pro prospect who could have been drafted in the later rounds of the NHL draft. I'm sure, however, they didn't circle my name the next time they came to see me play.

I have seen this scenario happen a number of times at the NHL level. A player is called up from the minors to the big club and plays exceptionally well for a short period of time. After a number of games, when the player starts to relax or feel comfortable in his new surroundings and the work ethic declines, the player doesn't play at the level required. Sooner or later, he is sent back to the minors. This doesn't happen all of the time, but I have seen it on many occasions. Few stay and develop into stars. Some stay and become good hockey players. Some stay and play a role on their team. Many others play great for a short period of time, then play average or poorly and are sent back to the minors. This is another example of how important it is to be mentally prepared for each and every game.

My decline started the following weekend on Friday night as we travelled on our bus from Windsor to Kitchener to play the Rangers. Early in the season, prior to my arrival, the enforcer on the Rangers hockey club had taken a cheap shot at Diego and knocked his two front teeth out. Diego wanted revenge and the rest of the team was willing to back him up. The plan was for Diego to cross-check the

Kitchener enforcer in the face during the pre-game skate, then pound him with his fists for as long as possible. This would, of course, initiate a pre-game brawl. In the dressing room prior to the game, many of the older guys were kidding around about who they wanted to fight. A number of the rookies, including myself, looked worried, although none of us would admit to it. I remember one of the older guys telling us rookies, that we shouldn't worry, that everyone would be looked after. If anyone were losing a fight, one of our teammates would jump in and assist.

That evening there were very few fans in the arena, one of the largest rinks in the league. It also appeared as if the lights had been dimmed, providing an eerie atmosphere. Kitchener arrived on the ice a couple of minutes after us. I should point out that there are no referees on the ice during pre-game warm-ups. As both teams circled the ice, I noticed Diego making his way toward the Ranger enforcer. He caught up to him just behind one of the nets. I was at the other end of the rink, circling the net, when everything happened. Diego cross-checked the Kitchener player in the face, threw his gloves off, and started punching him.

As I raced towards the other end of the rink, I noticed that most of the players had already paired up and that only one or two Kitchener players were alone. I skated to the first of them and grabbed his arm as tightly as I could. He was probably six feet three inches tall and about one hundred and ninety-five pounds. Needless to say, he was much larger than me. In addition, he had this look in his eyes like he was ready to start throwing punches. For the first twenty seconds, except for the occasional glance at me, all he did was hold onto me and watch what was going on around us. We both noticed, directly behind us, that our goalie had the Kitchener goalie down on the ice and was pummeling him with punches. The Kitchener player holding onto me quickly let go and jumped on top of our goalie. I just stood there for about five seconds – things were happening so fast. What was I supposed to do? I skated over and pulled the Ranger player off our goalie.

I don't know what happened after that with the two goalies, but as the Kitchener player and I locked arms again, one of the bigger players on our team approached us. He was holding onto a Ranger player who was my size. Within seconds we had switched players and I was now holding onto a Kitchener player who was my size. We looked at each other and then looked around at all the other players on the ice and began to have a pleasant conversation, although we were both ready to assist any one of our teammates if needed. He told me how he had just joined the Kitchener club and how much he enjoyed playing junior hockey. He also told me that he was not a physical player and didn't enjoy fighting. I was content to talk to this player and felt I had contributed to the brawl by assisting my goalie when he needed help.

The incident had a negative effect on my play from that point on and was one of the reasons my performance began to deteriorate. I had always felt that some fighting – two guys agreeing to square off – was part of the game. I did not agree with the bench-clearing brawls and the line brawls that were very much part of the game during the 70s and some of the 80s. I believed, and still believe, that hockey is a game of skill and should be adjusted to allow more offence. It's okay to have one or two enforcers on each team to ensure no one physically abuses their teammates, but when I played Junior, it appeared that almost every-one was prepared to fight, night in and night out, if they had to. I wasn't prepared to do this. I had no problem with the physical play along the boards and in front of the net, even though I lost most of those battles due to my size. But I was turned off by the war-like atmosphere of hockey at this level.

As a normal boy growing up, I got into several fights and won my share of them. I was never one to look for a fight, but somehow I seemed to get myself in the middle of things without trying. The following incident was typical.

One Sunday afternoon, my brother Frank and I were playing outside with some of our cousins at a family party in Toronto. Frank and I were about thirteen and fourteen years old respectively. A group of guys, probably around our age, started harassing us from across the street for no apparent reason. They kept calling my brother and me names because, and I can only guess, they didn't recognize us from the neighbourhood and were probably trying to impress someone. It takes a lot for me to get mad enough to actually fight so, being the oldest boy out of all the cousins there, I crossed the street and tried to talk to the guys who were harassing us. They were all over my brother for some reason. This just made things worse. When I tried to reason with them, they seemed to get more belligerent. Finally, as I began to leave, the guy who seemed to be in charge, and was a little bigger than me, pushed me from behind. I got up and, without throwing a punch, had him pinned to the ground in a matter of seconds. I got up and walked away without saying a word. They didn't bother us after that.

I knew I could take care of myself, but an incident at a

high-school football game changed my outlook on fighting, off and on the ice.

It was Grade 10. My friends and I attended one of our school's senior-team football games. We were members of our school's junior team, and were watching the senior team beat one of our archrivals. After the game, we were confronted by some of the bigger guys from our archrival's junior team. Some pushing and shoving took place and a number of us started pairing off. Before anything started, cooler heads prevailed and we agreed to settle things on the field the next time we were to meet. As we started to walk away, one of the other guys from the opposing junior team grabbed me, pulled out his knife, and told me that the next time this happened I was dead meat. By the look in his eyes, I knew he wasn't kidding. This kind of situation is more prevalent today and is the main reason not to look for trouble. I got into one or two other fights that were provoked by the *other* guy after this incident, but I tried to avoid fighting whenever possible. I was always concerned that the other guy might have a weapon.

In hockey, one of our players in Junior B had a seizure when he slipped and hit his head on the ice during a fight. All of the above, including the Kitchener incident, and the fact that I was a lot smaller than most of the other players at the Junior A level, contributed to my views on fighting.

The incident in Kitchener reminded me that the game of hockey had become a business and a war. It was not fun anymore. I started to look at the game differently. I became more aware of the surroundings and the environment. I became more aware of the other team's best and worst players and their enforcers. I became more aware of who I was battling for possession of the puck. Some of these things could have been channelled in a positive direction, but I began to channel them in a negative direction – I began to play cautiously. I began to *think* the game too much instead of letting some things happen naturally.

The bottom line is that I didn't believe that fighting should have a major role in the game of hockey and that belief affected my day-to-day performance.

 **LESSON # 20**

It may be impossible to change your point of view regarding fighting in hockey. If you are not naturally a fighter, work with a teammate or a professional in order to be prepared when the situation occurs. Practise the art of holding onto an opponent's arms and sweater so that it will be difficult for him to free his arms and start punching. Strengthen yourself with a weight-training program, which will also give you more confidence in other facets of the game. Work at defending yourself so that you are prepared.

— · —

The second cause of my decline had to do with my girlfriend at that time. She never gave me ultimatums or grief about my commitment to hockey, but she was not supportive. She was very indifferent to my hockey career and never seemed to be proud of my hockey accomplishments. She didn't understand that it's important to bond with the other players on the team, on and off the ice. She would get upset when I wanted to go out with my teammates for a night. Because my commitment was not as strong as it should have been, I gave in to her wishes and rarely went out with the guys on the team. It really didn't matter that much to me until I started playing with the Generals. She didn't attend the first home game against Sault Ste. Marie. She chose to go to the school dance instead and I met her there after the game. I was disappointed that she didn't attend because it was important to me that she show her support for my hockey career. I believe a supportive girlfriend should go to the game and then accompany her boyfriend to the dance after the game.

The next sign of trouble appeared when I told her that I had accepted the Generals' offer to play with their hockey club for the rest of the season. She threatened to break up initially, then, after reconsidering, changed her mind. I was not about to say no to the Generals and yes to her. She changed her mind almost immediately but it told me where her head was at. I should have broken up the relationship right then and there.

Then there was the issue of complimentary tickets. Every player on the team received two complimentary tickets, which we would usually distribute to parents, relatives, billets and/or friends. I gave my parents one ticket and my girlfriend the other ticket. The problem was that although my girlfriend attended almost all of the games, she usually didn't show up until midway into the second period or sometime into the third period. It infuriated my parents, who thought it was a waste of a ticket.

It wasn't my girlfriend's fault that my focus wasn't on hockey. I believe she could have helped me by being a lot more supportive and proud of my accomplishments. I allowed these things to happen and have only myself to blame.

LESSON # 21

It's important that priorities are maintained at all times. I am not suggesting that you shouldn't have a girlfriend, but if she is not supportive or proud of your accomplishments, it will have a negative impact on your hockey career, and possibly on other aspects of your life. Some guys will say outwardly that their girlfriends are supportive even though they know deep down that they are not. Be honest with yourself. When you reach this level, hockey and education should be your main priorities.

— • —

The third cause of my decline, and probably the biggest, stemmed from my overall work ethic. As you grow older and wiser, it's easier to understand that sacrifice and hard work are required in certain situations in order to achieve success. Most teenagers don't understand this. The ones who do will succeed and the ones who don't will probably not succeed. I made progress by recognizing what was required and by working hard to achieve my goals.

As the game became more physical – faster and harder – I didn't elevate my work ethic to match the overall intensity of the game. I wasn't prepared to sacrifice my body and do whatever it took to play hockey.

During the week, the Generals would practise every day after school for about an hour and a half. This was mandatory. Usually no one was on the ice before us so some of the players would get onto the ice about an hour before practice started. Some of the guys clowned around, but others worked on their weaknesses. Often they'd line up a number of pucks in the opposition end and fire shots at the net, trying to pick a particular target. Some players would partner up, with one being the passer and the other a shooter. Both players would have the opportunity to practise their passes and their one-time shots. I think I took advantage of the opportunity for extra ice time on only one or two occasions. I should have used this extra time to work on my weaknesses.

 **LESSON # 22**

Work hard during practice. Practise and play hockey with the same intensity. By not giving a full effort in practice, you may pick up bad habits that may appear during a game. Practice means just that: working on things that may improve you and your hockey team. Practice is extremely important. Guys who usually practise hard and work on their weaknesses are usually the players who succeed. One easy way to impress a coach is to always work hard in practices.

— • —

A number of coaches, probably all of them, won't tolerate players who don't give one hundred percent effort in practices. I was one of those players who, for the most part, went through the motions in practice. I hated to practise. It was boring and hard work, especially after a loss. I remember one practice with the Generals during which we didn't see a puck for the entire time. A lot of former hockey players reading this book are probably shaking their heads because they understand exactly what I mean. We did skating drills for the entire practice, and the drills made us feel like our lungs were about to explode.

The fourth cause of my decline was that I chose not to be part of the team. It was my fault and nobody else's. I chose not to attend team off-ice functions and not to spend some time with the guys on the team. I didn't have to spend every minute with the guys, but I should have gone to team off-ice functions on at least a bi-weekly basis.

In the past I had been perceived as a leader and was one of the players that most of the guys wanted to hang around with. One of my better qualities was that I would never try to alienate teammates just because they were either quiet or different. During my minor-league years, I always made time to be with my teammates by either coordinating or just simply attending off-ice functions. These were team-building experiences. They gave the players time to bond and get to know one another off the ice. It's a fact that the teams that spend a good deal of off-ice time together are usually successful.

With the Generals, I never gave my teammates a real chance to get to know me. I felt like an outsider and played like an outsider. I was never really part of that team. After practices, I would be one of the first players to shower, dress, and leave as quickly as I could. Some guys would stick around and either chat in the dressing room or go out for food or drinks. After home games, some of the guys would either go out for food together or go to a night club. Again, I was one of the first to leave to go out with my girlfriend and some of my friends from high school.

On the bus, rookies would have to share seats and were usually seated near the front of the bus close to the coaches, trainers, and any media. We were free to roam around the bus and socialize with the veteran players or other rookies, especially during those long road trips. But I would usually stick to myself and stay in my seat. During road trips where we stayed overnight, there were a few occasions where I went out with the guys, but they were few and far between. I remember on a number of occasions when team functions were announced in the dressing room. The captains always tried to persuade everyone to attend. I usually declined the invitation. Needless to say, a number of my teammates were not pleased.

LESSON # 23

Make a concerted effort to be part of the team. Socialize with the guys after practice and after games when possible. Plan to attend team functions on a regular basis. Interact with the guys on the bus and during road trips. This will have an impact on the way your teammates treat you and how you play the game of hockey. Have fun with your teammates.

— • —

One of the few times I ventured out with the guys, our team paid for it the following night when we got hammered by Sault Ste. Marie.

We arrived in Sudbury sometime around 11 p.m. Most of the guys agreed to unpack and then go down to the lounge for a drink or two before going to bed. For some reason, I agreed to go along. Things were lively in the hotel and before I knew it, I was with three of my teammates and a group of girls. The bar closed at 1 a.m. that morning and we went to one girl's home for more fun. It was after 3 a.m. when we got back to the hotel. The next day we travelled from Sudbury to Sault Ste. Marie and lost by a large margin to the Greyhounds. Our entire team, including myself, played poorly that evening.

My ice time slowly started to decrease as the second half of the season progressed. Instead of being one of the key players on the team, I was relegated to playing on the third or fourth line. My productivity, goals, and assists began to dwindle as well. I would go through several games without a single point. I became more and more frustrated and less interested in playing. The passion and intensity in my game no longer existed. I was simply going through the motions.

My first experience at Maple Leaf Gardens playing against the Toronto Marlies (they are no longer in the OHL) was uneventful. Since childhood, I have been a Toronto Maple Leafs fan. Like so many of their followers, I have supported the Leafs through the good times, but mostly through the bad times. Playing at Maple Leaf Gardens was supposed to be a dream come true. It ended up being quite a disappointing experience.

It was a short forty-five minute bus ride from Oshawa to downtown Toronto and Maple Leaf Gardens. We parked behind the arena, unloaded the bus, and made our way to the visiting team's dressing room. Unfortunately the room for visiting juniors was not the same dressing room used by visiting NHL teams. The room was extremely small and cramped. It was like minor-league dressing rooms all over again.

It was a thrill to finally skate onto the same ice as all of my favourite Leafs have done over the years. I spent the majority of the pre-game warm-up and game looking around in awe. The game was very disappointing. With just over one thousand fans in attendance, the arena appeared to be dark, gloomy, and extremely quiet. The atmosphere was poor and so was my performance. I spent most of the evening watching the game and looking around at the arena instead of playing hockey. We lost that game.

The playoffs were to begin and we would be facing the Sudbury Wolves in the first round. It was to be a best-of-seven series, with the Wolves having home-ice advantage. I saw limited ice time. We split the first two games of the series, with both teams winning at home. Game 3 was played in Sudbury before a capacity crowd. This game proved to be crucial as Sudbury began to dominate us physically and gain momentum.

Early in the game, Tom, our best player, took a stick above the eye from the Sudbury player who had been shadowing him. He did not return for the rest of the game. Due to Tom's absence, my ice time began to increase. I had very little impact on the outcome of the game. You'd think that I'd have relished the opportunity to make a difference and perform to the best of my ability. The fact is, I just got by. As with most things in my life at that time, including school, I was doing just enough to get by. We lost the game and now trailed in the series 2-1.

The game didn't end without incident for me, however. Midway through the second period, as I passed the Wolves goaltender to chase one of their defenders around the net, their goalie butt-ended me on the top of my nose. I fell instantly to the ground as blood started to flow onto the ice. It didn't hurt that much but it did shake me up. The trainer quickly attended to me, brought me back to the bench, did some of his magic, and soon had me ready to get back onto the ice. It was quite an experience for my mother, who listened to the entire incident on the radio back home in Oshawa.

Later in the game, in retaliation, I tried to slash their goalie, but every time I got close to their net, a Sudbury defenceman was there to steer me away. I had to time my retaliation properly, otherwise I could have started a bench-clearing brawl. I did take a few extra cracks at their goalie that resulted in a lot of pushing and shoving, but that was as close as I got. After the game, the Sudbury doctor closed up my nose with five stitches.

Game 4 was held at the Civic Auditorium in Oshawa. This was a must-win for us, because losing this game would put us down three games to one in the series, heading back to Sudbury for Game 5. Tom was not available to play, due to the injury suffered in the previous game. This again meant more ice time for me.

Early in the game there was a scramble in front of the Sudbury net. The puck squirted onto my stick and before I could think about where I wanted to shoot the puck, I slid the shot wide of the open side of the net. It was an opportunity that I should not have missed. A third of the net was vacant, since the Wolves goalie lay sprawled on the opposite side of it. I had reacted too quickly.

Midway through the second period, another opportunity to score occurred. I was flying down the ice, carrying the puck as I approached the Sudbury blue line. After a give-and-go with my winger, I found myself skating towards the goalie all alone. I faked to my right and went to my left. I had the goalie fooled as I slid the puck towards the middle of the open net. Just as the puck was about to cross the line, their goalie dove back and stopped the shot with his stick. I had missed another great chance to score.

LESSON # 24

Shoot the puck at the net with authority each and
every time. Even when you think there is no way the
goalie or defender can get back to stop your shot,
always take your best shot. Even when you have beaten
the goalie and he is sprawled on the ice, make sure
you try to raise your shot to score in the upper
half of the net.

— • —

Early in the third period, with Sudbury leading by a
goal, another scramble took place in front of the Wolves
net. Again, I was left unattended at the far side of the net
as the puck squirted towards me. This time, the puck was
definitely bouncing but I had half of the net open. I took a
couple of whacks at the puck until I finally made contact.
The puck trickled by the wrong end of the goalpost.

We lost the game, and eventually the series, four
games to one. In the local Oshawa paper the day after the
fourth game, there was an article describing the game. At
the end of the article there was a line that read, "Enzo
Augimeri missed three open nets." The statement was a
little exaggerated, but I should have at least scored on one
of the opportunities. Season over.

I had made up my mind at the end of the season that I
was going to give trying to become an NHL hockey player
a real shot. I was going to dedicate most of my summer to
working on my weaknesses, getting into great condition,

and becoming stronger. My intentions were admirable. The first thing I did was join a fitness club located adjacent to the Civic Auditorium. My plan for the latter part of May and the first half of June was to work on becoming bigger and stronger. The latter half of June, July, and August would be focussed on running long distances and sprints. This was to build my stamina and endurance. In early August I would start skating again, and by the end of August, the plan was to be on the ice three times a week.

Let me repeat, my intentions *were* good. I did go to the gym four times a week for about three weeks and then probably about once a week for the remainder of the summer. Going to the gym four times a week for about three weeks added a little bulk and strength, but nothing close to the amount required. I did run periodically over the course of the summer, but probably more like three times a week instead of the minimum five times per week required. Those runs were usually light jogs that covered maybe two or three miles at a time. On the program recommended by the Generals, by the end of the summer we would be running approximately five miles at a time within a specific period of time.

The real problem was that I did not skate, not even once, throughout the whole summer. I don't know what I was thinking, but I did not skate at all. Getting ice time over the course of the month of August in Oshawa or the surrounding area was not an issue. There were many conditioning camps and many opportunities to play shinny, but for some reason I chose not to skate. I spent the entire summer working part-time and hanging out with my girlfriend and friends.

Over the course of the summer, the Generals decided to make a coaching change and hired Jake, who had coached the Sault Ste. Marie Greyhounds the previous season. I met Jake the night prior to training camp at the arena as we received our equipment and our training-camp schedules. He was pleasant and made it extremely clear that he was ready and anxious to start the season.

Training camp began Friday morning with off-ice conditioning testing. We gathered at the civic stadium right beside the arena. After a number of stretching exercises, we were required to run twelve laps of the track, or three miles, within twenty-one minutes. I finished in a time of just over twenty-two minutes, which wasn't that bad but was not within the required time. Most of the players, veterans and rookies, made it within twenty-one minutes. The few of us who didn't, and there were a few veterans in that group as well, had to try again the following morning. The worst part of failing the first test was that this was my new coach's first look at me. And this was just Part 1 of Jake's first impression of me as a hockey player. He didn't have to say that he was disappointed with my lack of fitness – his look said it all. It's a common fact that players must report to camp in good physical condition. If I were him, I would have been thinking that this player was not committed.

LESSON # 25

Physical preparation during the off-season is extremely, and I mean extremely, important. Gone are the days when players used to play themselves into shape during training camp. The off-season is the time to work on your weaknesses and be better prepared for the following season. Consult with your coach, trainer, and/or a personal trainer on a recommended training program. Ensure the program is geared towards hockey, and that it includes weight training, aerobic, and anaerobic training. Work on your skating and other weaknesses in your game by attending conditioning camps and/or hockey schools. You can be prepared and become a better hockey player by working on your game during the off-season.

Having said that, my opinion is that all kids should take a complete break from hockey for a period of time after the season. Kids who are thirteen and under do not need to be actively involved in a summer league throughout the summer. Attending hockey camps on a weekly basis, or a hockey school for a one- or two-week period, is good. Players can work on certain hockey skills taught by certified instructors. It's important that kids get involved with other activities, especially in the summer, and to have fun, so that their focus is not entirely on hockey. I have seen a number of kids quit hockey because they continued to play year round and got "hockeyed out."

— • —

The afternoon following the morning fitness run, I stepped onto the ice for the first time in over four months. As we circled the ice and stretched to prepare for the upcoming scrimmage, I felt very awkward and uncomfortable. My feet seemed extremely heavy; it felt like I was skating in slow motion. In addition, I was getting winded quite easily.

As I lined up for the opening face-off at centre ice, I noticed that the opposing centre man was Greg, our first-round selection in the junior draft that summer. His seat in the dressing room was located right beside mine and we had chatted briefly before the scrimmage. As the referee dropped the puck, Greg dropped his gloves and jumped on top of me and started throwing punches. Luckily for me, he never connected and lost his balance. I quickly jumped on him and grabbed both his arms, but before I could start throwing punches, the referees were there to break things up. My performance from that point forward was awful. I had performed very poorly throughout the entire training camp. Part 2 of Jake's first impression of me was complete. I had failed the first test.

 **LESSON # 26**

First impressions last forever. It is very difficult to change someone's first impression of you. Make sure you are prepared for your first performance in front of your new coach. Work as hard as you can to ensure you impress upon him that you have an excellent work ethic, and that you are prepared to do whatever it takes to win. Be in top mental and physical condition. A coach's first impression sets the tone for how he views your approach to the game.

— • —

The rest of the weekend went just as badly as the opening scrimmage. For some reason, I was the only veteran to play in our opening pre-season game against Peterborough in Oshawa. I was so concerned with my performance and the possibility of not making the team that I met with the coach to get some feedback. He agreed that training camp had not gone well for me and told me that it was obvious I had not prepared properly over the course of the summer. But he was very optimistic. He told me to work hard and eventually things would work out. I left his office feeling quite relieved and made a promise to myself that I would do whatever it took to make the team.

As the pre-season drew to a conclusion, we played Niagara Falls in Oshawa. I played my best game, scoring a goal and assisting on another. After the game as I was leaving the dressing room, I saw Jake walking towards me. I asked him if my performance had improved. He told me that I had played well and that I had made significant improvement since the last time we had talked. My response was extremely inappropriate and, even though nothing was ever said about it, I know it caused some tension between management and me. I told Jake that the previous season, the media were made aware that I had not made the team prior to Vince talking to me face-to-face. From Jake's reaction, I knew I had put my foot in my mouth.

He looked shocked but at the same time, he gave me a very cynical smile. I had not only insulted Vince but the expression on my face must have given Jake the impression that I was extremely bitter. I also asked him to tell me my fate first, prior to advising the media. I did not handle the initial part of my relationship with Jake very well.

LESSON # 27

Never make negative comments about management to other management staff. If you disagree with something a coach or manager says or does, take a professional and business-like approach. Speak to that person in private and tell him in a calm and professional manner exactly how you feel. Keep an open mind, and be prepared for an honest and open discussion. This will help you get things off your chest so they do not fester. Most management staff will have greater respect for you because you were honest and forthcoming. It also gives them an opportunity to explain to you their point of view.

— · —

After three weeks of nervous anticipation and thinking the worst, I made the team as the Oshawa Generals' fourth-line centre.

The first game that season occurred in Sault Ste. Marie on a Friday evening. This was a special night for Jake because he had coached the Soo team, the Greyhounds, the previous season. We did not disappoint our new coach and defeated Sault Ste. Marie 6-3. I had four or five shifts per period and ended up with one assist. I missed a golden opportunity to score in the second period when I walked in all alone from the slot and fired a shot right into the goalie's midsection. My performance was mediocre at best.

We did not play again until the following week. We were scheduled to play in Windsor on Thursday evening and then in Kitchener on Friday evening. We lost in Windsor – I didn't play very well at all. The following evening in Kitchener, I played well, but not spectacularly, and we trailed by a wide margin after two periods of play. On my first shift in the third period, I skated like I had never skated before. For some reason, my legs felt as light as a feather and I played with an added zip and flair that was not evident in any of the previous games that season. I controlled the play and played with a sense of confidence and determination. I even scored late in the game on a slap shot from just inside the blue line. I was disappointed with the loss but upbeat that I had played my first good period of the season.

Two days later on Sunday evening, we were to face the Windsor Spitfires in our season's home opener. I was looking forward to playing the first game of the season in Oshawa because a number of my friends and relatives planned on attending the game. In addition, the home opener usually meant a big crowd and that always motivated me. Early that day, I started to prepare mentally by focussing on the little things that I had to do to perform well. I was also trying to get as motivated as possible because I knew that at some point, if my play did not improve, not only would I receive limited ice time, but there was a chance I might not get to play at all.

Game time in Oshawa was 7:30 p.m., and we had to be at the arena no later than 6 p.m. to have ample time to stretch and get dressed for the pre-game warm-up, which started at 7 p.m. I arrived at the arena before 6 p.m. and ran into one of the guys, Mike, just as I was about to enter the dressing room. He took me aside and told me which three players were "healthy scratches" (players who were healthy but would not be playing). Mike was one of them, and so was I. I thought, this is not really happening! I was a veteran player and deserved the opportunity to play in the home opener! Without any hesitation, I circled the corridor of the arena and went directly to the management office. As I knocked on the open door of the coach's office, I noticed one of the veterans, who had just arrived back from NHL training camp, talking to the coach. I had a very determined look on my face and asked Jake if I could speak to him. My teammate left the room as I sat down in front of Jake's desk. I asked him politely why I wasn't dressing for the game, and told him that as a veteran on the team, I was surprised that I wasn't playing in the home opener. I guess I wanted him to feel bad about his decision because I went on to tell him that a number of my friends and family would be attending the game. He reminded me that hockey is a game of numbers, and that he was giving the other players who had not dressed for the opening game in Sault Ste. Marie an opportunity to play. He was very positive and told me to keep working hard.

I did not argue with him but told him that I was disappointed and, that as a veteran, I felt I should have been playing in the home opener. Jake appeared to be somewhat uncomfortable and tried not to focus on my performance but on the fact that it was some of my teammates' turn to play. I kept my frustration in check. I didn't want to get mad at Jake even though I thought he was being extremely insensitive and was deliberately not playing me because I reported to camp in poor physical condition. As I walked out of the dressing room, I felt embarrassed. Now I had to face my friends and family. Looking back at this particular situation, I realize that Jake was right. I had not played well up to that point, and some of the rookies had worked hard and played extremely well. However, I thought his timing was wrong, I was just getting my confidence back and would have made the most of the opportunity to play in the home opener, especially in front of family and friends. I do think Jake may have been trying to send a message to me that I needed to work harder on a consistent basis. However, he should have told me exactly why I wasn't dressing. I left the room embarrassed and confused.

Even though coaches are not psychologists, they need to understand that each player is different and should be motivated differently. I didn't need a kick in the butt. What I needed was a tap on the shoulder and some words of encouragement. Benching me for the home opener was not the way to motivate me. I took it as a slap in the face, and instead of working harder, I became bitter towards Jake.

LESSON # 28

When you play at a competitive level of hockey, ice time must be earned. Equal shifts and equal ice time amongst players no longer exists. Being a veteran does not necessarily entitle you to certain privileges. Play hard and earn your ice time. Most good coaches will play the players who are performing well in practices and during the games. Remember, although other players on your team are your teammates, you are competing against them for a job and ice time.

— • —

I had not earned the right to play in our home opener since I had played only one good period out of the first three games (nine periods) of the season. The hard part about what had transpired was that I felt I was beginning to get some of my confidence back. Playing with confidence is extremely important and, even though the coach was right, not playing in the game was a big blow to my confidence.

There were few highlights in the forty games I played that season. I played with very little drive or confidence. I didn't take the bull by the horns and work hard to prove that I belonged, but just went along for the ride. My perception of Jake, who I had liked and respected, began to deteriorate, and it seemed nothing I did was good enough. Every time I had a good game, I would be a healthy scratch the following game. It was a confidence killer.

We played three games in three nights one weekend, with the first game against Sault Ste. Marie in Oshawa. I scored two goals that night and was a factor all night long. My two goals were not very pretty but I did something that you need to do to be a goal scorer. I planted myself in front of the opposition goal, took the usual abuse from their defencemen, and scored two "garbage" goals. The goals, and my performance, had no effect on my ice time; I only played four or five shifts a period. My dad, who was very critical of my play that season because he knew I could play better, thought that I had played my best game of the season.

The following evening, we travelled to Peterborough to play against the Petes. I was very excited and had a renewed sense of confidence because of my previous night's performance. When we got to the rink, the coach posted the line-up for that evening's game. I was shocked to see that I was a healthy scratch. I couldn't believe it. I had played well the night before and felt like maybe my game was finally coming around. I stayed to myself in the stands that evening and avoided my coach and general manager after the game because I was afraid I was going to say something that I would regret later.

The one game I will never, ever, ever forget was a game played against the Sudbury Wolves in Oshawa the following night. I was centring the fourth line, and played with our enforcer and another teammate who had a great deal of potential but was not having a very good season. He had been relegated to our line.

I played with drive and determination that night. I was going through people instead of around them. I played as if I was six feet four inches tall and two hundred pounds.

I thought I was Superman and no one could take the puck off of my stick. Early in the first period, on my first shift in a scoreless game, I raced into the Wolves zone. I battled vigorously with one of their biggest defencemen and managed to outmuscle him for the puck. I drove towards the net with another Wolves player draped all over me. I managed to shake him off and slid the puck to my teammate in front of the net, who scored our first goal of the game. I had another two or three shifts in the first period and played with the same zest as my first shift. We had a few good chances but didn't score. I was extremely disappointed that I did not receive additional ice time based on the way I was playing. My frustration with our coach continued to mount.

The second period was a carbon copy of the first as far as my performance was concerned. Near the end of the period, I stole the puck from one of the Wolves just inside their blue line. I skated hard towards the near corner of the rink and managed to muscle my way around the defenceman, who was attempting to body-check me against the boards. As soon as I got by the defenceman, I noticed one of my teammates gliding through the slot. I approached the side of the net and pretended that I was going to go around the net with the puck. As I started going around the net, in one quick motion, I rifled a pass to my teammate who was gliding through the slot. He one-timed the pass and scored high into the top of the net. Most people didn't realize that after I sent the pass in front of the net, a Wolves player gave me a solid check that lifted me right off my skates and flat onto the ice. The great part about the play I had made was that I knew I was going to get hit. I had sacrificed my body to make the play! But when I went back to the bench, our coach never gave me the sign of approval. Usually after a goal or a good play, most coaches acknowledge the effort by saying something or tapping you on your butt or helmet. I was now past frustrated and very angry.

The second period ended and I made my way back to our dressing room. I realized that I had played only three or four shifts the entire period. I had reached a boiling point and could not handle my frustration any longer. I grabbed our captain and took him into the stick room, located across the hall from our dressing room. I began to vent my frustrations before we even closed the door. Fortunately, he understood that I wasn't venting at him but at our coach. I let him know that I was furious because no matter how I played, it was just never good enough. He tried to calm me down, but before he knew it I started crying. Yeah, that's right, crying. I was very good at handling my emotions as a teenager, but for some reason, everything just came wailing out. He calmed me down, and I apologized for breaking down. I think he really did understand that I must have been extremely frustrated to start crying. That incident did not change a thing. I don't know if our captain talked to the coach but my ice time did not change over the next week or two.

One night in Kingston, I was on the ice for one of my rare shifts. With the limited ice time, it was hard to get the legs going for the first part of the shift and I had to ensure my mind stayed focussed as well. I took a pass near our blue line and as I turned around to move forward, one of Kingston's forwards caught me with his shoulder and sent me back-first to the ice. I lay there in shock and in pain for about ten seconds. I had just taken a thunderous check and had the wind knocked out of me. I heard one of our defencemen yelling "Get up, get up!" I slowly raised myself off the ice and headed directly towards our bench.

LESSON # 29

Keep your mind focussed on the game at all times. Whether you get one or twenty shifts a game, watch and pay attention to what is going on. Try to keep your body, especially your legs, loose on the bench at all times. Your one shift per period, or one shift per game, may be your only opportunity to show your coach that you deserve more ice time. In addition, when you are on the ice, keep your head up. There are always players on the other team waiting for the opportunity to administer a devastating body check.
If you don't keep your head up, you can't see what's coming your way.

— · —

A couple of weeks went by and things remained the same. I usually played in two out of every three games and was a healthy scratch in the other game. One afternoon as I entered the dressing room for practice, a lot of the guys who were there already had very serious looks on their faces. You could feel the tension in the air. Our trainer advised me that we had made a trade. We had traded two of our defencemen and a centre to the Windsor Spitfires for their goalie, one of the premier goalies in the league.

The centre who was traded played a little more than me, but was one of the guys I had been battling with for regular duty. I was shocked by the deal because two of the guys who had been traded were very popular players in the dressing room. The deal gave me a renewed sense of enthusiasm, both because they didn't trade me, and also, it gave me an opportunity to have more ice time.

Our first game after the trade was against the Toronto Marlies at Maple Leaf Gardens. The stage was set for me to have a great game. I was playing at Maple Leaf Gardens, the home of my beloved Leafs. Our coach juggled the lines for this game and I was centring the third line with two good wingers.

I played a very good game that night and received a fair amount of ice time. With the game tied very late in the second period, Jake put my line-mate and me onto the ice with both teams one man short. This was the first time all season that I had been on the ice with both teams not at full strength. I made the most of my opportunity. I won a key face-off and, after some play in the Toronto zone, I passed the puck in the slot to my line-mate, who scored.

In the third period, with our team now with a big lead, I broke out of our end with the puck and eventually scored on a pretty give-and-go with a teammate. I jumped into the air and celebrated like I had scored my first goal in the league. I was excited because I wasn't scoring many goals that year, I had scored in Maple Leaf Gardens, and many of my relatives were in attendance to witness the goal. After I had finished celebrating, I went back to the bench and waited for the public address announcer to announce my name as the goal scorer. It didn't happen. In fact, he incorrectly credited the goal to our defenceman and didn't even credit me with an assist! You can only imagine how badly I felt. They did eventually correct the score sheet and I was credited with the goal. Unfortunately, they never announced the correction.

Again, my play that evening in Toronto didn't change the amount of ice time I received. The combination of my inconsistent play and our coach's intentions to play me on an irregular basis continued. For a period of time, I was getting extra ice time just to take key face-offs. I had developed a reputation as one of the better face-off players in the league. One evening in Oshawa, we were trailing the Kingston Canadians 2-1 with less than a minute remaining in the third period. I lined up in the Kingston zone to take a face-off against Tim, who would eventually move on to have a good NHL career. Tim was not only good at face-offs, but he was also six foot four, two hundred and twenty pounds. He may have been one of the strongest guys in the Ontario Hockey League.

I won the draw, and one of my teammates managed to get a good shot on goal. The goalie made a good save. The second face-off occurred in the same face-off circle as the first one, to the right of the net. This was to my advantage, as it was easier for me to draw the puck to my backhand. I won the draw again, cleanly, and passed the puck to our defenceman back at the point. He took a good shot that was stopped by the goalie. The puck was directed right back onto my stick. I reacted quickly and shot the puck towards the low corner of the net. The Kingston goalie stretched out his glove as far as possible and made an amazing save. I won the third face-off and we eventually scored the tying goal. We won the game in overtime and I assisted on the winning goal. Two games after that night against Kingston, I was a healthy scratch, watching instead of playing.

I want to relay an extremely frightening incident that occurred during a game. We were playing the Ottawa 67s in Oshawa in a rare Saturday afternoon game. Because it was a Saturday afternoon, we had a good crowd with a lot of kids in attendance. I was on the ice in the second period when a fight broke out right in front of our bench between one of our players, Steve, and one of the tougher Ottawa players. I was standing about ten feet directly behind Steve. After several punches were thrown, the two players became entwined and proceeded to wrestle. The Ottawa player obtained the advantage and eventually wrestled Steve to the ice. Steve didn't fall lightly and wasn't able to break his fall since his arms were wrapped around the Ottawa player. His head hit the ice hard. His helmet cracked immediately upon impact. He turned over towards me and I saw his eyes roll. He was bleeding from the back of his head and started having convulsions. His whole body was shaking. There was complete silence in the arena.

Without hesitation, our trainer jumped onto the ice, as did the team doctor, who was seated right behind our bench. They eventually managed to stop the convulsions, got Steve onto a stretcher, and wheeled him off the ice into an ambulance. I visited Steve in the hospital that evening. He had a concussion and had received numerous stitches to the back of his head. It was a frightening scene that stayed etched in my mind for weeks.

As the trade deadline approached, my frustrations continued to grow. In addition, my love and desire for the game of hockey had soured. I was no longer motivated during games, and especially not at practices. I was going through the motions and everyone knew it. I made up my mind, after consulting with my parents, that the only way to get my career back on track was to ask for a trade. The next day after practice, and only two days before the trade deadline, I talked to Vince, without Jake in attendance, and asked him for a trade. He seemed to think that my request was a big joke. He assured me that he would try to trade me but I had left it to the last minute. He had a smirk on his face during our entire conversation that made me feel uncomfortable, and led me to believe that he wasn't being totally honest with me.

Two days later, the trade deadline passed and I remained a member of the Oshawa Generals. A couple of days after that, we added an over-age player who had previously played with the Generals. Guess what position he played? That's right, he was a centre. My fate was sealed.

My days as an active member of the Oshawa Generals were drawing to an end. At least in my mind, there was nothing I could do that would change the management's mind about my abilities and my role on the team.

Over the next few days, I pondered my future with the hockey team and my aspirations of becoming an NHL hockey player. I weighed my options and gave it a great deal of thought. My desire to become a pro hockey player had died. I was completely frustrated with the game I had loved as a kid. I felt like my back was against the wall and my hands were chained to it. If I played poorly, I would not dress the following game. If I played well and started to gain some confidence in my game, I would still not dress for the following game. My manager barely talked to me, and when he did, he talked down to me. In my opinion, he wasn't being honest with me, and had me stereotyped as a fourth-line player who wasn't good enough to play every game.

My decision was made and I had decided to take the easy way out. I quit. I really did. I quit the Oshawa Generals hockey club. I made two major mistakes in my hockey career; this was the first. Instead of working harder and proving everyone wrong, I took the easy way out and quit. The problem was that my heart wasn't into it. No matter how hard I tried to talk myself out of quitting, I was not ready to make the necessary commitment to resurrect my hockey career.

LESSON # 30

Quitting may appear to be the easy way out, but in the long run, you are just running away from your problems. Face the music and stand up to the people you need to stand up to. Be honest, open, and diplomatic. The only thing you learn from quitting is that every time you face adversity, you are going to run away from your problems and quit. Every time you quit, it becomes easier and easier. Taking the easy way out never works. Finish what you start.

— • —

I arrived at the next practice early and tried to sneak my skates out of the dressing room before anyone could see me. But the trainer saw me and took me aside. He knew what I was doing and told me that I was making a big mistake. I let him say his peace, thanked him for everything he had done, and went to see the coach. I told him that I was quitting the team. He offered little resistance, although he did appear concerned and questioned me on my motives. I told him that I had lost my desire for the game and that no matter how well I played, it was clear his opinion of my play would never change. He offered no rebuttal. I left the coach's room and felt like the world had been lifted off of my shoulders. I thought my problems were solved. I didn't realize that I was quitting the team for the wrong reasons. Even though I still believe Jake did not handle me properly, the blame for my downfall rested squarely on my shoulders. I did not show the heart, commitment and desire to compete on a consistent basis. I played lazy most of the time and wasn't willing to work harder to prove to Jake and Vince that I had the ability to play at the Major Junior A level.

I went directly home and told my parents. They were extremely disappointed and tried to convince me that I was making a big mistake. I knew they were right, but I felt that if I were to continue playing hockey I would become more frustrated and it would start affecting other aspects of my life. In fact, it already had. I was miserable day in and day out. I had lost confidence in my ability to play hockey and my self-esteem had been bruised. It was time to move forward with my life. That evening, I visited my girlfriend and the first words that came out of my mouth were that I had quit the Generals. She didn't believe me at first but eventually did. She seemed quite surprised but didn't try to talk me out of my decision.

A week after I quit the Generals, my father visited Coach Jake to discuss my decision. I met with both of them one afternoon in the coach's office. It appeared that the Generals were willing to take me back. My father had a long discussion with Jake, who explained that one of the reasons he was not playing me was that I had reported to training camp out-of-shape. It was obvious that when he made his line-up decisions, my poor work ethic would always come to mind. To be fair to Jake, there were other factors, including my indifferent play throughout the year and my less-than-100% effort in practices. I told them both that I was not interested in returning, and that after a few games, I would be back watching the games as a healthy scratch. I was not willing to embarrass myself by returning to the team and then not playing.

Life without hockey was something I was not used to. I had been playing competitive hockey ever since I was five years old. I was now eighteen and my evenings were free to do whatever I wanted with them. I felt lost and unsure about my future. My dreams had been shattered and I really wasn't sure what I wanted to do with my life. I studied a little harder, but for the most part all I did was hang out with my girlfriend and my friends. My parents weren't happy with my new-found freedom.

As the months passed, I became extremely bored with the additional time on my hands and began to miss hockey. I started to think about applying for a hockey scholarship at an American university. I contacted United States International University in mid-May and was advised that they had filled their roster and were no longer interested. I called a few schools in Michigan and Ohio, but either they were not interested or they had never seen me play. I was resigned to the fact that I was going to play with the Oshawa Legionnaires Junior B hockey club and would try to get a hockey scholarship to the U.S. the following season.

The vice-principal of our high school, Mr. Cole, was very strict but fair. A number of the students in Grades 9 and 10 were afraid of him, but as I got to know him over the years, I realized he was a very good man. He had followed my career and was interested in helping me get a hockey scholarship in the U.S. He had played at the University of Michigan when he was my age and knew the coach of the Wolverines. He sent the coach a letter outlining my career, recommending that they recruit me. A few weeks later, I received a three-quarter scholarship to attend the University of Michigan in Ann Arbor. A three-quarter scholarship meant that the university paid for tuition, books, and a room. My only responsibility was meals and, of course, spending money.

I don't remember if I ever properly thanked Mr. Cole for sending that letter. It was one of the nicest things that anyone has ever done for me. I hope he reads this book because this is my way of saying "THANK YOU."

Prior to signing the contract to attend Michigan, I visited Ann Arbor and the campus with my father and my Uncle Italo. We were treated extremely well, and stayed at one of the nicer hotels in downtown Ann Arbor. I was a big fan of college football. I had admired the University of Michigan Wolverines because of the proximity to Toronto and because they had cool helmets. On our tour of the university, we entered Michigan Stadium where the Wolverines played football. I will never forget walking onto the field and standing at the fifty-yard line. The football stadium seats over 100,000 fans, but it didn't look that big from the field. I was awestruck by the surroundings and stood there for the longest time with my eyes wide open and my jaw probably resting on the ground. I will never forget that experience or my first game as a fan at the stadium.

CHAPTER SEVEN

The U.S. Hockey Experience

University of Michigan

I was ready to start a new journey, revitalize what looked like a dead career, and begin new dreams. But my work habits still had not improved. I only worked semi-hard over the course of the summer. I ran (enough to get by), lifted weights (again, enough to get by), skated (enough to get by), and partied with my friends over the course of the summer. What troubled me was that there would be high expectations because coach David and the rest of the coaching staff had never seen me play. My scholarship was based on the letter from my vice-principal and possibly some research that they had conducted. First impressions were going to play a major part in their evaluation of me as a person and as a hockey player. I did prepare, but not as much as I should have. I was in reasonably good shape. If I had arrived in Ann Arbor in very good or great shape, that would have obviously made a difference.

My parents, along with my sister and my girlfriend, drove me from Oshawa to Ann Arbor. We arrived sometime early afternoon at the dormitory that I would be rooming in. I completed all of the necessary paperwork and made my way to the fourth floor, using the stairs, and located my room. I had never been inside a university dormitory before. I had been living in Oshawa in a very large, clean (my mother made sure there wasn't any dust in the house) four-bedroom house. My room in Oshawa was almost the size of the dormitory room, which I would be sharing with a roommate who had not arrived. The room had bunk beds located directly to the right of the door, two small desks, half a fridge, a sink, and two closets with drawers. The washroom, which had a number of shower stalls, was located about thirty feet down the hall from my room. The dorm room was obviously not a five-star suite, but it was a regular dormitory room and it was fine.

We all went out for an early dinner and then came back to the dormitory. My parents dropped me off at the front doors, said their goodbyes, and started on their journey back to Oshawa. There I was, all alone in a university town. I didn't know a single person except for the coach, who I would visit the following day. I went back to my floor, made my way down the hallway, and introduced myself to a number of the guys. I met a couple of guys who were part of the gymnastic team, and in the last room at the end of the hall, I met a member of the tennis team and a highly recruited freshman who would be playing with the basketball team. I got a fair bit of attention because I was different. I was CANADIAN, and a member of the university hockey team. That made me one of the most popular guys on our floor.

The following day I registered for a number of courses and went to see the coach to let him know I had arrived. There are rules and regulations in the NCAA as to when training camp can begin, so camp didn't start until a week after I arrived. My roommate arrived that night, and let me tell you, we were complete opposites. Bob was a good guy but his philosophy on hockey, school, and life in general was completely different than mine. He was a partier and it was crystal clear that we were at school for different reasons. However, we hit it off initially and for the first five consecutive nights we went out and had a good time. Okay, we went out drinking. We partied. We weren't stupid, but we had lots of fun. The differences between us started to become more evident when training camp started. I was willing to tone down the fun during the week and focus my attention on hockey and my schoolwork. Bob, on the other hand, wanted to continue to party. He would often get home extremely late, sleep in, and miss his classes. For the most part, I made sure to attend *most* of my classes.

I was better prepared for the off-ice conditioning programs that season. I had done enough training during the summer that I was able to finish the one-mile run in less than six minutes, and the five-mile run in the allotted time. I did not spend enough time weight training but was able to get by. The only problem I had was that American beer is different than Canadian beer. I wasn't use to it, and since Bob and I had consumed a considerable amount in the first week, my stomach was upset for the first week of training camp. On-ice sessions went well, and I could see out of the corner of my eye that all of the veteran players were watching me as I performed each drill. We played a couple of exhibition games against some local teams that were not in our league. I played okay but felt, as I assume others did, that there was plenty of room for improvement.

Our first game, and my first experience of U.S. college hockey, came a few days later on a Friday night against Bowling Green University. I didn't dress and I really can't remember if we won or lost. As I recall, Kelly, a highly recruited freshman and the brother of an NHL hockey player, was the only freshman to dress that evening. The rest of us, including a few veterans, watched from the stands. The atmosphere was fun and electric. The fans were involved and vocal throughout the entire game. A band played at every stoppage of play. They would play the university theme song, or a popular song, or a song that somehow mocked the opposing team. I didn't think twice about not dressing for the game. I had a great time and it was quite an experience.

The following evening we played our first home game at Yost Arena (our home rink) against Bowling Green University. I was in the lineup, playing on the fourth line. I played a good, but not great, game. It was a different game from junior hockey and I had some trouble adjusting. There is no centre red line in college hockey, which opens up the game. Junior is more of an NHL style of play, with a great deal of play up and down the wings and dump-and-chase hockey. College hockey appeared to be more of a wide-open game, with less physical play. In addition, we were all required to wear face-masks on our helmets, which seemed to eliminate fighting for the most part. Late in the game, with our team leading by a number of goals, I broke in all alone on the goalie. He made the initial save, but I managed to put the rebound behind him and score my first goal for the University of Michigan.

As we made our way into our dressing room after the game, I was still pretty excited about scoring my first goal. Our assistant coach, Darryl, who had watched the game from the press box, quickly brought me back to earth. Before I got to my locker, he took me aside and sternly told me that I needed to improve my defensive play if I was to stay in the lineup. I politely agreed with him and went to my locker. What a jerk! I thought. I knew he was right, but his timing sucked. He could have waited until Monday's practice to properly point out my defensive deficiencies. I was not thrilled by his comments but did not let them negatively affect me that evening. This was my first experience with Darryl, but not my last.

The following weekend we were scheduled to play games against Western Michigan University at Ann Arbor on Friday night and at their home rink on Saturday. My parents came down for the weekend. Since I was away from home for the first time for such an extended period of time, it was great to see my folks.

LESSON # 31

Appreciate the sacrifices your parents make so that you can play hockey. Although most of them enjoy the experience, they sacrifice their free time, wake up early to drive you to practices, leave work early, use vacation days to accommodate your schedule, and, most of all, make a large financial commitment. They do this for you. Spend time with them and show them you love them. They are special, and no one can ever replace them.

— • —

One of the most special aspects of my Ann Arbor experience was the university band playing the Michigan theme song, "Hail to the Victors," every time we skated onto the ice to start the game or a period. No matter how I felt, in the mood or not in the mood for the game, that song definitely gave me an emotional lift.

That Friday night, against Western Michigan University, the theme song was played as our team, the Michigan Wolverines, skated onto the ice. I was sky high, having worked hard in practice to ensure I would have a spot in the lineup that weekend because my parents would be at the game. I played on the fourth line with Kelly and another line-mate, and knew that my ice time would be limited. On my very first shift, after eluding the defender, I skated hard for the net, received a pass, and steered the puck into the open side of the net. As I rounded the corner in celebration, I saw my father smiling. My parents had arrived just in time to see me score.

We won that night and the following evening in Kalamazoo, Michigan. I was starting to establish myself as a fourth-line centre. This was fine by me because most freshmen in the league rotate in and out of the lineup. I was ready to earn my way to the top. I realized that I would have to prove to the Wolverines that I was good enough to play on a regular basis, and once that was achieved, I would work on moving my way up the ladder. Things were finally starting to go my way. I had scored two goals in the first three games that I had played and thought I would be playing on a regular basis as long as I continued to play well. As usual, things were about to change.

I arrived ready to practise the following Monday after my last class. The players that had arrived earlier were seated in their stalls in the dressing room, still in their street clothes. They were advised not to change into their hockey equipment until everyone had arrived and after the coaching staff had met with everyone. Darryl, the assistant coach, conducted the meeting without our head coach, David, who was not present. Darryl advised us that David had apparently become quite ill, and that he, Darryl, would be taking over as coach for the remainder of the season. We were all in shock. David was a very good man and all the players liked him. We were starting to gel as a team early in the season with David behind the bench. I was taken off-guard by the news because of my first experiences with David and Darryl. David was always pleasant and easy to deal with. Darryl, on the other hand, had made that ill-timed comment to me after my first game. I was extremely apprehensive about him taking over.

One of the problems I faced right away was that Darryl's practices were harder than David's. *Much* harder. But, when I think back to Darryl's practices, they were well-planned and they were good for our team. He made sure that we were well prepared, mentally and physically, for the weekend games. To be fair, there is nothing wrong with working very hard in practices. Because I didn't like to practise, I didn't work as hard as I should have. I'm sure Darryl noticed that my work ethic during practices was not very good.

 LESSON # 32

Develop a positive relationship with your coach. Work hard during practices and in games to earn his trust. Keep the lines of communication open. Just because a coach may get emotionally wrapped up in a game or situation and says something derogatory to you, it doesn't mean he has lost his faith in you. Don't be so fragile. Suck it up, and learn from the experience. Different coaches have different coaching styles. Learn to be adaptable and adjust to your coach's style. Learn from the feedback that is provided to you. Almost all coaches want you to do well. If you do not adjust or adapt to the team game plan or the coach's philosophy, you will either find yourself watching from the stands or from the bench, or being released or traded.

— • —

Not only was I not working as hard as I should have in practices, I was not buying into the coach's defence-first philosophy. I had always been an offensive player who did not pay enough attention to defensive zone coverage. This had been part of my problem with the Oshawa Generals. My focus was never in the defensive zone. Darryl was happy to win games one to nothing, two to one or three to two. In my mind, I was second-guessing the coach and the style he wanted our team to play. Who was right? Obviously the coach was right. I spent too much time focussing on things that were out of my control. I should have worked extra hard during practices to learn defensive zone coverage. I spent some of the next several weekends in and out of the line-up until after Christmas, when I managed to establish myself as the fourth-line centre.

One of the most controversial issues in university or college hockey over the years has been the ritual of initiation, or "hazing," as it is termed in many circles. I had been initiated with both the Oshawa Legionnaires and the Generals, but nothing very interesting happened. My experience with the Michigan Wolverines, on the other hand, is definitely worth telling.

I was having dinner with friends at a restaurant one Sunday evening when a couple of the guys from the hockey team showed up. As soon as I saw them and the smirk on both of their faces, I knew exactly what was about to happen. With very little resistance, I accompanied them to a house located on campus that was occupied by four or five of the seniors on our team. Most of the freshman (rookies) were in the backyard with the rest of the team. We played a number of drinking games that only the freshmen took part in. I guess we could have refused to participate, but we were "strongly encouraged" by our fellow teammates to drink. The freshmen, including myself, were not about to balk at a ritual or tradition that is part of junior and college hockey.

As we all became drunk, the veterans started the shaving process. I happily went along with everything that came my way. Three of us got what was called "special treatment." Since Kelly and I were the freshmen that were playing the most, after the drinking and shaving had been completed, we were taken out of the house together. We were quite drunk at this point and could have been talked into doing almost anything. We were "asked" to remove all our clothes. We were then blindfolded and seated on the front hood of a teammate's car. A teammate held onto each of us as the car slowly started motoring along the campus roads. We were paraded around the entire campus at a very slow speed so that onlookers could get a bird's-eye view. This lasted for about fifteen or twenty minutes until we finally came to a stop in front of one particular building. We were thrown onto the ground as they poured maple syrup all over us. Once the maple syrup stopped, they put small sponges on us that stuck to the syrup.

The guys walked us up a number of steps, took off our blindfolds, and knocked on the door. If you haven't guessed it yet, this was a girl's sorority house. As soon as the door was opened, our teammates disappeared. The girls who opened the door screamed and, as we walked into the house, there were ten or fifteen other girls standing and watching. Some were laughing and some were shocked, while others pretended not to look. (You know who you are.) I was extremely relaxed about the situation and could have taken the opportunity to meet some girls but instead I was more focussed on getting the heck out of there. A couple of the guys at the house, visiting their girlfriends, got us each a pair of shorts and kindly escorted us out. We were drunk and had no idea where we were. We started running down the streets of the campus, and finally figured out that we were about ten minutes away from our dorms. A police officer stopped us at one point and asked, "What the heck do you guys think you're doing?" We told the officer what had happened. He laughed and sent us on our way. We asked him for a ride but he just laughed, saying that he didn't want to mess up his car.

We made it back to our dorms without incident. The other teammate who received special treatment was an older player who had made the team for the first time as a senior. What was special for him about the initiation was that he was raised in Ann Arbor and knew a lot of people in town. At the same time Kelly and I were being escorted around the campus, our teammate was being escorted in the same manner. The guys stopped at the main campus bar, brought him inside, sat him on a bar stool, ordered him a drink, took off his blindfold, and left him there, completely naked. Our teammate handled this incident with complete composure. Apparently, he stayed on his bar stool, chatted with other patrons, and finished his drink before heading home.

We were all in stitches the following day when we heard what had transpired. Our laughter didn't last long because we heard about a dangerous incident that had occurred the same night. Apparently, another player who had made the team but was more of a practice player, had also been initiated. Some of the guys had driven him to his dormitory and dropped him off on the front steps. His roommates found him, out cold, and took him to the hospital. He was suffering from alcohol poisoning and was in very bad shape. He did recover, but the incident made the front page of the Detroit newspapers and became a national story.

Our hockey team was suspended from going to any of the bars in Ann Arbor for the entire hockey season. In some circles, this may not seem like much of a punishment, but to our hockey team, it was harsh punishment. For the entire hockey season, I don't recall of any of us entering a bar on campus.

 **LESSON # 33**

Hazing, or initiating new teammates, is a ritual that occurs with most junior and college hockey teams. Have fun, but be responsible. The above is a situation that may be the extreme, but issues can occur. The younger players look up to the team leaders. Show some leadership and take responsibility for the initiation process. If things are getting carried away, stand up to your teammates and take charge to put things back into perspective. Ensure that the rookies don't drink too much, and make sure that they get home safely. Again, have some fun, but be responsible.

— • —

I had a great deal of fun attending college and playing hockey in the U.S. that year. I matured and became more independent. I had to keep my dorm clean, ensure that I had three meals a day, and wash my own clothes. However, I was extremely homesick and lonely up until Christmas. After Christmas, as I started playing more and hanging out with the guys on a regular basis, things began to change and I started to really enjoy the experience. Not going to a bar on weekends after games didn't dampen our spirits. A typical home weekend would consist of the following:

- Practice on Thursday after classes
- Team dinner at a nice Italian restaurant (sure beats cafeteria food!)
- Game 1 Friday evening
- Team dinner at a restaurant after the game
- Game 2 Saturday evening
- Party at one of our teammates house – start around 11 p.m. and last all night
- Get back from party Sunday morning between 5 and 7 a.m.!
- Wake up before 1 p.m., on time for cafeteria lunch
- Watch NFL football all day
- Study Sunday evening

I also managed to do well in school, maintaining a B average. I focussed on taking many business courses but also took a speech and psychology course. I was always a good student, but never exceptional because I was busy with hockey, and also because I never studied as much as I should have. I do remember that I actually stayed home on a Saturday evening while in Michigan to study for a psychology test. I memorized all the necessary terms and aced the test the following week.

The University of Michigan is rich in college football tradition. They were consistently ranked as one of the top twenty schools in the country year after year. It was exciting for me to attend my first football game at Michigan Stadium early in the school year. The weather was not very cooperative on that Saturday afternoon as light rain turned into a steady downpour. I sat with most of the guys from our team, in the end zone at one end of the stadium, in the student section. The Wolverines were playing Northwestern University, one of the worst teams in college football at the time. The game was really close until Michigan scored a late touchdown to win. I guess what blew me away was that there were 106,000 people watching a terrible opponent (who played extremely well that day), in the rain. That was a special season for the football team since they beat their archrivals Ohio State in Columbus and went on to win the Rose Bowl.

During my hockey career, I had the opportunity to play in a few NHL arenas. I played at Maple Leaf Gardens in Toronto, the Quebec Collisée in Quebec City, and the old Olympia in Detroit. During the Christmas break that year, I played in the GLI, the Great Lakes Invitational tournament, held yearly at the Joe Louis arena, home of the Detroit Red Wings. As with my initial experience at Maple Leaf Gardens, we beat Michigan State in the opener and I spent most of my time watching instead of playing. I did get a regular shift on the fourth line but I was in awe of the crowd, some 17,000 spectators, and of the fact that I was playing on an NHL rink. I had a great chance to score during the game. I received a pass in front of the net, about 15 feet from the goalie, but he stopped my shot easily.

We stayed that night at an expensive hotel in Detroit, down the street from the arena. We played Michigan Tech the following afternoon in the final. They were one of the top-rated teams in the country at the time. The game was low-scoring and was tied at two at the end of three periods. As overtime dragged on from period to period, my ice time seemed to increase. It wasn't because I was playing exceptionally well but because we were all getting tired and everyone was taking shorter shifts. Finally, in the third overtime period in front of more than 18,000 fans, Michigan Tech scored and won the game and the GLI tournament. I played two average games but should have been at my best. The atmosphere in the arena was electric. There were two bands playing at each game. More importantly, there were a number of NHL scouts. I should have been at my best to help my team win and to make a good impression, both on our coach and on the NHL scouts in attendance.

LESSON # 34

The expressions "could have," "should have," and "if only" are for losers, not winners. Give your best when the occasion demands it. Don't lament after the game that you could have or should have played better. Put your best foot forward when the opportunity arises, and not after the fact. No matter how tired you are, you can always summon up a bit more energy. Start what you finish and always give your best, right up until the end.

— • —

After scoring two goals in the first three games of the season I went without a goal until late in the season, when I scored my third and last goal in Minnesota. In between goals, there were games that I watched from the stands, games that I played okay in, and games that I played well in. One of the assistant coaches once told me that if I worked on my skating and got stronger, I could be a force in the league. Both of the assistant coaches were good guys and they encouraged me to do well.

Things were going fine until I was promoted to the first line for weekend home games against the University of Minnesota.

My Uncle Italo, his wife, my Aunt Corinne, and my mother were scheduled to attend the Saturday night game and spend the night. This was going to be a great weekend, since my mother was going to see me play on the top line against Minnesota, one of the top ranked schools in the country. The first challenge was to play well in the Friday night game to ensure that I would stay on the top line for the following evening's game. I played extremely well. I worked as hard as I could that night and was rewarded with a lot of ice time. I managed an assist on our line's only goal of the game. The night went extremely well, except for one important fact – we lost the game 6-2. Why is this important? No matter how well some players play, the fact that the team loses makes some coaches make changes. Coach Darryl was one of those coaches.

I showed up very excited and ready to play the following night. I felt like I was going to play my best game of the season. As usual, prior to the pre-game warm-up, the coach announced the starting roster in order to ensure we practised on the appropriate lines. I was not on the first line. I was not on the second line. I was not on the third line. I was not on the fourth line. Yes, I was scheduled to play, but I was not on a line. I was confused. As my teammates made their way onto the ice, I approached the coach and asked him politely what line I was on. He replied that he wasn't sure where I was going to fit in that night, but to be patient and he would play me. This made me furious. I understood that we had lost the previous game, but in no way was it my fault. I went out for the pre-game warm-up and worked hard because I was extremely pissed off. All I could think about was that my mother, uncle, and aunt were going to make the five-hour drive from Toronto to watch me sit on the bench.

Fifteen minutes into the first period, the coach finally tapped me on the shoulder for my first shift of the game. I played well on that shift, and on the three or four other shifts per period I received for the rest of the game. Eventually I was back on the fourth line and stayed there for the rest of the game.

With about eight minutes left in the third period and our team trailing by three goals, my winger received a penalty. Our line had been on the ice for only ten or fifteen seconds, so we weren't tired. Normal shifts would last anywhere from thirty to forty-five seconds. Our coach, apparently without hesitation, sent our penalty killers out onto the ice and our line was to come off. When the play had stopped, I was deep into the far corner of our end and had a long way to skate before I reached our bench. What did this mean? It meant that I had too long to think about being taken off the ice and also about what had happened over the last two days. By the time I reached our bench all I could think of was how much of a @#$%@#$% our coach was. To my mind he had crossed the line. He was closer to the other end of the bench when I ripped into him. As I started to sit down, I looked him right in the eye and told him that he was a &*%@#$#@$. I said this quite loudly; most of my teammates on the bench heard exactly what I said. They were in shock and so was I. I couldn't believe I had uttered those words, and that I had uttered them in front of all my teammates.

The coach came up behind me and started to lose it on me. He started screaming and yelling, and told me to get off the bench and go to the dressing room. He said this about four or five times until he finally started focussing back on the game. I just sat there and pretended to ignore him. I decided the best thing that I could do was to just sit there and apologize for my actions after the game. After the game, I went directly into the coach's office before even taking off my hockey equipment. Obviously he was still quite upset and was not thrilled to see me. Before I could apologize, he told me that I was suspended for two weeks and not to show my face at the arena until then. I tried to apologize again but was told to get out.

The suspension lasted about eight days. I went to see the coach the Monday after the following weekend. He was very receptive and we had a nice chat. I apologized for my behaviour and I was reinstated on the team.

 **LESSON # 35**

I think the lesson here is quite obvious.
You may remember that a similar situation occurred
when I played minor hockey. Do not second-guess, yell,
scream, or get mad at the coach at any time, especially
in front of your teammates or the coaching staff.
By doing so, you are questioning his decisions,
philosophy, and authority. The coach is the boss
and makes the decisions on the bench.
If you disagree with what he is doing, and if this has
an impact on the way you and your team are playing,
then have a discussion with him in his office. Do not yell
and scream, but diplomatically explain your position and
listen to what the coach has to say. The key concept here
is that the coach is the boss. Never make him feel that
you are questioning his authority.

— • —

To my amazement, in my first practice back from the suspension, the coach placed me on the third line. I was as surprised as some of my teammates – not only was I dressing for the next game but I had been promoted to the third line. It didn't last very long. I played the first period on that line and then was back on the fourth line for the start of the second period. I don't know what the reason for this change was. I had been playing quite well but I wasn't going to challenge the coach's decision.

We made the playoffs, defeated the University of Denver in Denver two games to nothing, and then lost at Michigan Tech the following weekend. My roller-coaster first year of hockey at the University of Michigan was over. After the season ended, I focussed on having lots of fun and on my academics. I managed to attain a B average.

The day I left the University of Michigan for summer vacation, I stopped at the coach's office. I advised Coach Darryl that I had made a decision not to return the following year. He was quite surprised by my decision but did not make much of an effort to change my mind. The following factors influenced my decision:

- Lack of motivation to become an NHL hockey player – my heart just wasn't in it
- Coach Darryl's defensive-first coaching philosophy
- Coach Darryl's unpredictable decisions
- Coach Darryl's perception of my abilities
- Distance from family and friends
- Girlfriend
- I could transfer and play hockey at the University of Toronto.

This appeared to be sound thinking but I hadn't taken enough time to think about my decision. It was made in probably less than one hour, and without talking to family and friends.

Less than three weeks after decision day, I knew I had made the wrong decision and started to regret what I had done. I called Coach Darryl and told him that I had changed my mind and wanted to return the following season. He said that he had used my scholarship money for a new freshman and did not have any money for me. I didn't try to question his comments or argue his position, but just thanked him once again for the previous year. I had made the wrong decision again because I had not considered the following factors:

- Great new friends and teammates
- Wonderful learning environment
- First-class university
- Very good hockey program
- Challenge to excel
- Challenge to win Coach Darryl over
- Inexpensive way to obtain a university education
- Opportunity to further "grow up"
- Would not miss another year of hockey due to transfer rule
- I had a great time during the second half of the school year

LESSON # 36

Don't make rash decisions. Take the necessary time
to consider the pros and cons of your decision. Talk to
family and friends, especially your parents, and take into
account their feelings and positions on the matters being
discussed. Conduct any required research to ensure that
all pertinent factors have been considered. Once a
decision has been made, sleep on it. Most of the time,
you will feel the same way the following day, but
sometimes decisions may feel right one day and not
the next. The bottom line is, take the necessary time,
investigate your options, weigh the pros and cons,
and consider the opinions of others before making
a final decision.

— • —

NCAA and CIAU rules dictated that I was ineligible
to play hockey for the University of Toronto for one year
because I had transferred from the University of Michigan.
As a result, I didn't play any hockey the following year.
The year was also significant because at the end of it, my
girlfriend and I broke up. I saw it coming because we had
grown apart in many ways. I was bitter at first because we
had been together for five years and I had taken her
feelings into consideration when making some of my
choices. It was a difficult time for me because I had quit
hockey, again, and no longer had a girlfriend. Ultimately,
it was probably the best thing that could have happened

to me. She had never been very supportive of my hockey ambitions. My parents believed that my girl-friend was the reason I didn't devote more time to becoming a pro hockey player. Although there was some truth in that, the bottom line was that neither my heart nor my work ethic were geared towards a pro hockey career. Even today, when I think back to some of the decisions that I made, I may have been influenced from time to time by others, but if I had really wanted to become an NHL hockey player, I would have made the necessary sacrifices.

CHAPTER EIGHT

Having Fun and Getting Serious

University of Toronto

I received a phone call from Gord, the coach of the University of Toronto hockey team, prior to the end of the school year. He wanted me to play for the team the following year. I advised him that I had not played hockey for an entire year, but would consider his invitation and get back to him over the next couple of weeks. A week later, I called him and told him that I was interested in playing. At this point, I was looking forward to playing hockey just because I enjoyed playing the game and hanging out with the guys.

My attitude, my mindset, and my overall outlook on hockey had changed. I no longer felt the pressure of having to perform at my best night in and night out. I was a lot more relaxed on the ice and tried to have fun playing hockey. Even though I had had a great deal of fun at the University of Michigan, my year at the University of Toronto had to be my most enjoyable year of hockey for the following reasons:

- We had a very good team
  (ranked #1 in the country most of the year)
- Great bunch of guys
- Many team outings at U of T and on road trips
  that were a lot of fun
- I played on a great line – good
  chemistry right from the outset
- I led the league in scoring until I was
  injured in late January
- I met my wife while attending classes
- I had confidence in my game and I had fun
  when I was playing
- The coaching staff was good and fair

Training camp was held at Varsity Stadium for off-ice conditioning, and at Varsity Arena for on-ice conditioning. The one factor that was different than past camps was that I had played with four of the guys before. This made it easier for me to fit in with the rest of the guys. One of the players was from Oshawa, two of them played for the Legionnaires and the fourth played for a short period of time with the Generals when I was there. They were all older than me but they all made me feel quite comfortable. In addition, anytime you play well and are a key part of your club, other players tend to look up to you and/or accept you more readily.

Our first game was against York University at the annual University of Toronto hockey tournament at Varsity Arena. On our line's first shift of the game, I skated over York's blue line with the puck and took a low wrist shot that bounced off the post and into the net. It was a huge boost of confidence for me, especially since I hadn't played hockey at a competitive level in over a year. It was the start of many good things to come for me and my line-mates. We won the game and I added an assist on each of my line-mates' goals.

Our line became one of three very good lines on the team and eventually became the second power play unit. The difference between this team and others that I had played on was that we were a team that played both on and off the ice together. One of my fondest memories of that year was the socializing as a team at different functions when we weren't playing on weekends. Experts talk about teams that have talented players but don't win consistently, and that's because they may not gel and work together as a team. The best team always wins *as a team*, and not because it has the most talent.

My line had many great games throughout the first half of the season and I established myself as the leading scorer in the league. I was having fun playing hockey and the results spoke for themselves. Our biggest early season accomplishment came at a tournament held in Montreal in early November. All of the top ranked teams in the country were at the tournament, so it was a good test for our hockey club to see how we stacked up against these clubs.

We won our first three games and made it to the championship game. One of our wins came against the University of Moncton, the defending Canadian champions. Our line had made quite an impact in the first three games. We had scored a number of the team's goals, including three by me. We played the University of Saskatchewan and defeated them 6-3 to capture the tournament. I scored two goals and had an assist in probably my best game of the season.

After the tournament the rankings in the country changed. The University of Toronto Blues were now ranked number one in the country.

I met my future wife, Leena, prior to the Montreal tournament. Actually the tournament gave me an excuse to talk to her. I had been introduced to her in passing by a schoolmate one day in the hallway between classes. I didn't see her again for a week or two, until a couple of days prior to the tournament. I had just walked into class when I noticed Leena sitting at the end of an aisle beside an empty seat. I quickly made my way past a number of other students and planted myself beside her. We talked and before the end of class I asked her to take notes for me because I wouldn't be at the next class. I was going to be at the tournament in Montreal. She accepted, and the rest is history. The funny part of the story is that she wasn't a student in that particular class, but was there to meet another guy – a guy, in fact, who I had just passed in the hallway.

Leena was very attractive and had striking features. She had worked as a model and had minor roles as an actress in a few movies. I guess the thing that attracted me most to her was that she was extremely sweet. Although her clothes were kind of wild, I thought she was a good person with a smart head on her shoulders. I guess I was right because she now is one of the most renowned trainers and speakers in Canada on the subject of aggressive children under the age of twelve.

Late in January, during a regular practice drill, I took a pass near the opposition's blue line and immediately tried to pass one of our defencemen. He instinctively stuck out his knee and it collided with my knee. I flew across the ice and landed in a lot of pain. I crawled for about twenty seconds until our trainer came out to attend to my injury. I had torn the ligaments in my knee. This was a devastating blow. Our assistant coach later told me, probably to make me feel better, that I was the team's best player up to that point in the season. He didn't mean I was the most talented player on the team but I had performed better than the rest. I had never suffered a major injury in my career before so this was new territory. I was disappointed because I had been having a great year. Leena appeared to be as devastated as I was and offered me a great deal of support. Unlike previous years, I didn't quit but worked very hard doing exactly what the trainers advised me to do to recover as quickly as possible.

I attempted a comeback at the CIAU finals held in Moncton, New Brunswick nine days after the cast was removed. Early in the second period of our first game, I again collided with an opposition player's knee and strained the ligaments in the same knee. Career over. I was disappointed but not crushed. When I injured myself earlier in the year, I had a lot of time to think about my future in hockey. It was obvious to me that, even though I was having a great year, my dream of becoming a professional was remote. There are very few players that move on to the NHL from Canadian University hockey. I had matured enough to know that it was time to start thinking about career ambitions in the business world. The second injury made that decision a lot easier.

Leena and I were married in June 1985. We have two wonderful girls, Melissa, age thirteen, and Jessie, nine. They are a very important part of my life. My experience in hockey has taught me a number of valuable lessons that have helped me to deal with family and career issues. I have learned how to deal better with disappointment and frustration. I understand that some sacrifices may be necessary to achieve goals. The most important lesson I have learned is a need to communicate in all situations to ensure that I have a proper understanding of an individual or situation and that others understand me or my perspective. I used to make only about an eighty-percent effort in any activity; now I try and give it my best each and every time.

I sometimes wonder what it would have been like to be a pro hockey player, with all the fame and fortune that goes with it. I reflect on my hockey career at times and regret some of the decisions that I made. After I retired, some of the guys I played with or against in junior hockey were still playing. It was difficult to watch them, knowing that if I had put in the extra effort required, things might have been different. But I can tell you this, *things always work out for a reason*, and the reason for me is my wife and children.

 **LIFE'S LESSON**

Play hockey for the love of the game. When the game is no longer fun, it's time to look forward to other things in life.